Ernest Belfort Bax

The religion of socialism; being essays in modern socialist criticism

Second Edition

Ernest Belfort Bax

The religion of socialism; being essays in modern socialist criticism
Second Edition

ISBN/EAN: 9783337261542

Printed in Europe, USA, Canada, Australia, Japan

Cover: Foto ©Suzi / pixelio.de

More available books at **www.hansebooks.com**

THE

RELIGION OF SOCIALISM

BEING

Essays in Modern Socialist Criticism

BY

ERNEST BELFORT BAX

AUTHOR OF

" *The Ethics of Socialism*," " *Handbook to the History of Philosophy*," *etc., etc.*

SECOND EDITION REVISED

LONDON

SWAN SONNENSCHEIN & CO.

PATERNOSTER SQUARE

1890

„Wie Alles sich zum Ganzen webt,
Eins in dem Andern wirkt und lebt!"

Faust, erster Theil, Akt I.

THE ABERDEEN UNIVERSITY PRESS.

PREFACE.

A FEW introductory words may seem necessary in presenting the following pieces to the public in book-form. They have most of them already appeared in various periodicals (*Time, To-day, Commonweal, Justice*, etc.), and this fact will explain any repetition of idea or mode of statement which may here and there be discoverable, also their, to some extent, heterogeneous character.

The first article contains a condensed presentation of the cardinal points in the evolution of history. Such a statement must necessarily pass over many important details, and leave little room for illustration. The chief aim here has been to enforce the truth that the evolution of human society is a progress from Socialism *to* Socialism—from the simple, limited, tribal Socialism of early man to the complex universal Socialism already prepared in the womb of time. The treatment of this vast theme at a length which will admit of its approximately adequate discussion in all its bearings, is a task the author hopes to accomplish

in the future ; but at present the following brief instalment was all that could be given.

Other essays in the present volume touch upon the
same subject directly or indirectly. It cannot be too
strongly insisted upon that either the theory of modern
Socialism rests on a solid historical basis, or it is
nothing. The truth discovered by Marx, that the
basal factor determining the constitution of society
is its material and economic condition, must be for
the Socialist the key to the reconstruction of history.
Socialism, we contend, is not a theory "won from
the void and formless infinite" of Utopian sentiment
and good intentions, very beautiful, but impracticable,
as some think ; or from that of an aimless discontent
acted on by wicked and designing agitators, as others
think ; but it is a plain deduction from the facts of
history. The living form of Socialism has been long
perfecting itself within the chrysalis of Civilisation.
The process completed, nothing will prevent the empty
hull from bursting asunder and the new being from
issuing forth in its fairness and freedom. The more
repulsive, the more dead and withered, the harder in
outline the forms of Civilisation appear, the sooner
may we look for their final destruction. We often
hear of the taunt from middle-class thinkers and
writers, "I am no Revolutionist, I am an Evolutionist." This abstract way of looking at things is

characteristic of current *bourgeois* habits of thought.
To be an Evolutionist in the view of these gentlemen
is tantamount to being an anti-Revolutionist. The
notion of Evolution is erected into an absolute category, which is supposed to embrace the sum total of all
sweet reasonableness in social matters. Over against
this is another opposing category,—that of Revolution.
Just as Evolution is the sum total in *bourgeois* eyes
of all possible rationality, so Revolution is the sum total
from the same point of view of all possible irrationality,
—Ormuszd and Arhiman, the kingdom of light and
the kingdom of darkness. But the scientific Socialist
who takes a concrete view of things, unhampered
by the abstractions in which the current thinker is
immersed, fails to discover in the real world any
revolution that is not part of evolution, or any evolution that excludes the possibility of revolution as one
of its momenta.

The inability of the middle-class intellect to view
things otherwise than abstractly is not surprising,
seeing that our whole *bourgeois* civilisation is a system
of abstractions erected into independent existences.
In evidence of this we have only to look at the
existence of classes itself, each class being simply in
the last resort an embodied abstraction. Thus, out
of the distinction between the social functions of
direction and immediate production have arisen the

embodied abstractions of an upper, possessing, and
ruling class, and a lower, non-possessing, and ruled
class, within which moulds the conflict between individual interests as such, over social interests has
worked itself out, to the temporary victory of the former.
So with the subordinate classes within these classes,
each one is the embodiment of some *phase* of human
life, torn or abstracted from the rest, that is, from
the whole to which it belongs. The same with our
culture. In the specialisation which characterises
the learning of the nineteenth century, the basal
unity of knowledge is lost sight of, and each little
grovelling specialist thinks that in his own science
and its methods the fulness of knowledge is manifested. He despises philosophy, one function of which
is to reduce his speciality to a mere aspect of a larger
whole. His science is his philosophy, much in the same
way as the " public " of the ordinary man is his class.

The progress of the capitalistic system has tended
to render the economic bedrock of all things social,
increasingly evident, by reducing the super-incumbent
strata to a more and more rudimentary condition.
Hence the anachronistic absurdity of Conservatism.
We are not here referring merely to current politics,
. the rival parties of which are only too obviously of the
nature of business firms who trade in the emoluments
of office; but to the underlying principle which Con-

servatism may be supposed to have originally embodied. On the face of it Conservatism meant the desire of the decaying feudal or landed class to maintain itself against the rising middle or capitalist class. But in addition to this primary question of class interest, it is certain there was in many minds a genuine horror at the vulgarisation of life and the destruction of old-world sentiment and institutions, which they instinctively felt the ascendency of the capitalistic class to involve. Some had also, doubtless, a glimmering of the truth that "progress" in the middle-class sense did not mean a material betterment for the mass of the people, but rather the reverse. Such we may suppose to have been the sentiment which underlay (in some cases at least) the Conservatism of the Royalist side during the English parliamentary struggle of the seventeenth century.

But the work of destruction has now been done. There is no longer anything to conserve in the old sense. The aristocratic or landed classes of to-day are simply a wing of the "great middle class" in every sense of the word. Land itself is, in the present day, simply one of the forms of fixed capital. The landlord's sole aim is to obtain the greatest amount of surplus value in the form of rent from his land. The reciprocal duties of the mediaeval lord and tenant, their religious sanctions, and the sentiment they involved,

have passed away absolutely and completely. The
lord himself is more often than not a trader; he
invests the unconsumed portion of his revenue in
some business enterprise, and is invariably a shareholder in joint-stock companies, even when he is not
a promoter or director of the same. As such his
sympathies are as much with " improvements " in
machinery, with the extension of railways, the open-
ing-up of the world-market, and the spread of *bourgeois*
civilisation generally, as the middle-class *parvenu*
himself. It becomes more and more evident that we
have to-day but two classes in society,—the capitalist
class and the working class. The House of Lords is
simply a legislative body of capitalists possessed of a
special monopoly. The plea which the Conservative
of old had is, therefore, no longer valid. All that is
now to be conserved are the very things which to the
Conservatism of the past were the abomination of
desolation. The past that might have been conceived,
in a sense, as worth preserving, has already disappeared,
save for some tattered rags, befouled with the filth of
a world in which they are an anachronism and an
absurdity, and about the continuance of which no one
really cares. The true Conservative is, therefore, of
necessity as extinct as the dodo; and the modern
political Conservative is simply a " Liberal," or, in
other words, an upholder of the modern capitalistic

order, trading under another name. It is necessary
to point out these things, as there are occasionally to be
found Rip van Winkles, who, while bitterly hostile to
middle-class Philistinism in all its aspects, yet persist
in calling themselves Conservative. The Rip-van-
Winkleism in question is, however, it is to be
feared, too often no more than a piece of silly
affectation and *bizarrerie*.

Socialism is the great modern protest against
*un*reality, against the delusive shams which now
masquerade as verities. It has this at least, if nothing
else, in common with primitive Christianity. Early
Christianity affirmed that principle of absolute morality,
of individualism, of the mystical relation of the soul
to the supernatural, as the basis of religion, which
represented the real intellectual tendencies and aspirations of the period, in opposition to the established
but *un*real state-religion of the Roman Empire,
representing, as it did, the forms of things which
had ceased to be, viz., the old race-solidarity in communal and city life, and the naïve conception of nature
as directly personified. Similarly, Socialists to-day
affirm the principle of human solidarity through
the triumph of the cause of labour, *i.e.*, the real
interest of the modern world against the *bourgeois*
civilisation that professes to represent an economic
individualism which has ceased to be ; and against

its ethical and speculative counterpart, the introspection and supernaturalism, which have also ceased
to be as living realities. The great industry has
destroyed the last vestige of the one; science (using
the word in its widest sense) has destroyed the last
vestige of the other. But in both cases the dead
forms remain. The *bourgeois* moralist is never tired
of preaching the reform of the individual character
as the first condition of human happiness, ignoring
the fact, that science knows of no such thing as
an individual character, apart from social surroundings. He holds fast the old fallacious standpoint,
according to which individual good men make healthy
social conditions, rather than acknowledge the truth
that it is healthy social conditions which make good
men; in the same way that it is not great men
which make history, but (as is recognised by every
critical student of history in the present day) that it
is history which makes great men. The old super-
naturalist creeds drag on their meaningless existence.
Men are classed as Catholics and Protestants, Christians and Moslems, quite irrespective of their real
beliefs. By the conditions of their livelihood they
are bound to let it be supposed that they give their
adhesion to doctrines respecting which they have
not given an hour's thought in their lives, or which
they may actually despise in their hearts.

Socialism breaks through these shams, in protesting that no amount of determination on the part of the individual to regenerate himself, however successful he may be in cultivating the correct ethical trim, will of itself affect in aught the welfare of society ; that concern for the social whole is the one object of religion ; and that the placing above this of any abstract theological ideal, be it Christian, Mussulman, or Buddhist is (to employ the old phraseology) an act of apostacy. On this view the old theological questions, such as that of the continuance of the individual consciousness after death, may be interesting, but have no more *ethical* or *religious* importance than other interesting questions, such as that of the origin of the irregular Greek verbs, or of the personal or impersonal authorship of the Homeric poems.

In concluding (with apologies to the reader for having been seduced into extending what should have been an orthodox preface into something like an independent disquisition on Socialism), I will venture to express the hope that the present little volume may, notwithstanding the somewhat promiscuous nature of its contents, be not entirely without suggestiveness to those for whom Modern Socialism has an interest.

CONTENTS.

UNIVERSAL HISTORY
FROM A SOCIALIST STANDPOINT.

"ALL things flow," said Herakleitos, of Ephesus. Translated into modern language this is as much as to say, "The reality of any given thing is simply the temporary form assumed by the elements composing it." In the historical development of the world we find stretched out, on (if we may so speak) the procrustean bed of time, the different factors which go to make up our life and civilisation of to-day, no less than that of any other period on which we may choose to fix our attention. Every custom, every law, every religious belief or rite, our very thought, language, characters, habits, not to speak of our architecture, our clothing, our literature, which are their outward and visible expression, could, both severally and as a whole, be traced back and back into the night of the past, till lost in prehistoric times and primitive forms of social life. All this may sound familiar enough, and some may even be disposed to resent the statement of it as a platitude. Yet how few really grasp the great truth, that they and theirs, as they appear to-day, are but products of a long historic development. How little do they realise that, were they to go but a short way back

1

into the past, they would cease to recognise the
characteristics of modern society; that their most
cherished beliefs and practices, perchance, might
be found to take their origin from such as would
excite their keenest horror and indignation! How
little do they dream that their conceptions of
history, of past periods of civilisation, even when
they have any, are unconsciously coloured through
and through by the world they see around them!
The critical conception of history, for which history
is a succession of dependent social formations, one
born from the other; in short, the true notion
of human development as a continuity in diversity
is perhaps the most important and wide-reaching
speculative truth to which the nineteenth century
has given birth. Once we occupy the critical
standpoint, and we see history in a new light;
then, for the first time, we discern a meaning in
the often apparently capricious course of historic
events. (See Appendix, I.)

The method of historical sequence is based on
that of logical sequence, but with the difference,
that the abstract logical movement, as realised
on the plane of history, has to be discovered by
analysis and disentangled, so to speak, in its
several lines, from the unessential matter with
which it is encumbered. All growth or evolution
involves the notion of capacity unrealised, and
capacity realised; in the language of the schools, of
the potential and the actual, of the matter and the
form. The acorn is the unrealised capacity of the
oak, which is realised in the oak; the new-born
infant constitutes the capacity or possibility of the
full-grown man; the capacity present in the child
realises itself in the form of the man. But the
realisation of the capacity of a thing involves the
destruction or negation of the immediate or present

existence of that thing. Every step in the growth
of a child is a step towards the negation of
childhood. In proportion as the child progresses
towards manhood the less he is of a child. In
the man, the child, quâ child, no longer exists,
any more than if he were dead. In the realisation
of the perfection of the child's faculties his childhood is abolished. In the same way the oak-tree
presupposes the negation of the acorn; the acorn,
as acorn, wears itself out and breaks up; but the
moment of the destruction of the acorn is the
moment of the genesis of the oak. The same
process is seen throughout all life.

It appears, then, that growth implies a process
comprising three terms; the first, indefinite and
crude, with the seeds of its own negation present
in it as part of its very nature from the first;
the second, the accomplishment of this negation,
which accomplishment, however, becomes the matrix
whence issues the third and final term of the
process, which is nothing else than the negation
of that negation. Here what was latent capacity
becomes reality; what was potential becomes actual;
what was merely tendency becomes fact. But this
Dialectic does not lie on the surface of history
any more than on that of other planes of knowledge. The concrete world is a complex network
of many different lines, each working out its own
process; and in the entanglement of these lines it
is sometimes difficult to discover the central course
of development. As we have already pointed out,
we are not here concerned with the logical process
in its abstract and pure form. In history, as in
the real world generally, it may be arrested,
delayed, or modified in any particular instance,
without any infringement of the general principle.
A given seed, for instance, may die, or its vitality

be suspended for years ; or it may live and its normal development be diverted by some external cause. The aim and meaning of the philosophy of history is the discovery of the Dialectic immanent in it, of the main process underlying the whole development. For in spite of the complexity which seems at first sight so insuperable, we can undoubtedly discern a main stream of development embodying itself, during one epoch, in one group of races or peoples, and passing on perhaps in the next epoch to another such ethnic group, but maintaining itself through the diversity of the material in which it is successively realised as the same stream of tendency, a movement one and indivisible. (See Appendix, II.) Thus, in history as elsewhere, nothing passes away absolutely, since all that has preceded forms an essential part of all that follows,—a truth which, platitude as it may seem at first sight, can never be too assiduously borne in mind.

In the earliest period of human society man does not distinguish himself from the natural forces and objects around him. He conceives of nature as like himself animated and conscious, and hence as capable of being friendly or unfriendly towards him. In this stage, also, the individual man, as an individual, has not consciously distinguished himself or his interests from those of his fellow-men with whom he is associated ; in other words, he is completely identified with his social surroundings ; he lives simply in and for the society which has produced him. In consequence, all life, all work, all enjoyment, all government, is in common ; individual interests and individual property are unknown. The individual, in short, is completely merged in the race. This earliest condition of man as a social being

is what is sometimes referred to as Primitive
Communism. It is essentially the prehistoric era
in human development—that of the Lake dwellers
of Switzerland, of the men of the drift, and of
the countless ages which succeeded before chronology begins. Yet, although it is mainly prehistoric,
and therefore only to be reconstructed in imagination from its surviving traces in various parts
of the civilised world, or from the crude, imperfect
analogy afforded by the savage and barbaric races
of the present day, we find rich indications of it
in the world's oldest literary monuments ; in the
Homeric poems, the Icelandic sagas, the Nibelun-
genlied, etc. As regards the surviving traces of
its economical forms which we have spoken of,
existing like little oases in the arid desert of
civilisation surrounding them, we may refer by
way of illustration to the Russian Mir, the Swiss
Allemen, and the Hindoo village community, etc.
How long this primitive period lasted in undis-
puted sway we know not. All we know is, that
at the dawn of authentic chronology we find that
it has been long superseded by civilisation,—civilisation in the form of the ancient Oriental empires.
These represent the then highest phase of evolution, the dominating power of the world as the
curtain rises on the drama of history.

It is not difficult to see that the primitive
social formation is an instance of what Herbert
Spencer would term "the instability of the homo-
geneous." All the oppositions and antagonisms
expressed in civilisation are as yet latent; but
although latent, they are none the less present
and bound to manifest themselves in the end.
The first stage of human society is based on the
principle of kinship in its various gradations of
proximity. This notion of kinship of itself implies

an exclusiveness, an antagonism, which must sooner or later issue in civilisation, with its classes and races, and its class and race feuds. This, indeed, we may regard as the chief principle of change in prehistoric society, its chief solvent. It produced the earliest form of organisation,—organisation for military and predatory purposes. Hence the prominence of militaryism in all early civilisations ; it having been out of the necessity of organisation for offensive and defensive objects that civilisation first arose.

The term *prehistoric* as applied to the first period of social man has a deeper meaning than as merely indicating that we have no written records concerning it ; it may be taken to mean that the antagonisms, with the unravelling of which history is concerned, have not as yet manifested themselves. Nature was as yet identified with man, being regarded, that is to say, as a system of conscious beings like human society ; the individual was identified with the race. Hence the echoes of the prehistoric period,—the period, that is, preceding civilisation, either in the history of the world as a whole, or of any special people ·—present us with the dim and shadowy figures of gods and heroes moving across the stage, with scenes in which the processes of nature personified, stand for the deeds of human beings, and in which the movement or the custom of a whole people or tribe appear as the action of an individual man,—its legendary divine founder. This is what we call mythology. Prehistoric man, his · customs, and beliefs, is the material of myth. Time has as yet no significance, Myth knows no chronology.

History, I take it, can hardly be better defined than as the unravelling of oppositions ; the bringing to distinctness of latent contradictions, the

realisation in their conflict, of mutually hostile
tendencies. The oppositions wherein history—or,
which is the same thing otherwise expressed, the
development of the State, or of Civilisation,—
consists, may, I think, be reduced to two chief
pairs, i.e., *the opposition or antagonism between
Nature and Mind, and the opposition or an-
tigonism between the Individual and the Society.*
The first opposition spoken of, that between external nature and the human mind, is more immediately of speculative, religious, and artistic
significance; while the second, that between individual and society, of more immediately practical
interest. But they are intimately connected with
each other, and advance *pari passu.* In the
antagonism between individual and society is contained the notion of personal ownership of property, with the whole state-machinery which is
its expression. In the antagonism between nature
and mind is given religion, that is, religion in
the sense of supernatural or spiritual religion, as
opposed to the *naïve* nature religions of early
man. In the period of primitive communism and
that which immediately succeeded it, religion, it
must always be remembered, had for its end and
object the society; it was the idealistic expression
of the life of the society. Man was concerned
with nature, which he conceived as composed of
beings like himself, only in so far as it affected
the society,—the clan, the tribe, the people, etc.
With the progress of civilisation and of the reflec-
tive consciousness accompanying it, man separated
himself as a conscious being from nature, which
became henceforward inert matter for him, governed
by deities outside it. At a later period, wider
generalisation subordinated these deities to one all-
powerful conscious being, to whom they, as well

as nature, were subordinated. It was with this
being that man now concerned himself, rather than,
as before, with the processes of nature *per se*.
What interested him henceforward was the relation
of himself to this being. This became the subject-
matter of religion, which ceased to occupy itself,
as heretofore, with the life and movement of the
community. Religion, now gradually ceasing to be
social, became individual.

We have said that, what proximately led to the
transformation of primitive communism into primitive civilisation was race or tribal exclusiveness,
based on the notion of kinship, near or remote,
through descent from some common divine ancestor,
generally indicated by the possession of a common
totem,—a plant or animal specially sacred to the
clan or tribe. But within the historical period
itself, we can distinguish progressive stages, which
we shall see have been also determined by the
same principle,—a principle by which the transformation of one form of civilisation into the other
has been largely effected. The principle of political
exclusiveness has contributed to break down every
civilisation, thus paving the way for its successor.
Let us now glance at that social whole of prehistoric
times from which civilisation was a progressive
departure, but yet which left such deep traces
upon civilisation, especially in its earlier phases.
Early society tends to expand from its simplest
and closest form to others increasing in remoteness.
The foundation of society, alike in the order of
its nature and in the order of its history, is the
blood-family. Now the earliest form of the blood-
family may for practical purposes be identified
with that which Lewis H. Morgan terms the
Punalua family ; where ascertainable, blood-relation-
ship is recognised as precluding sexual intercourse,

or, in other words, in which sexual relations are
established on the basis of groups, from which
children of the same mother of opposite sexes are
excluded.* From this family-form the institution
of the *gens*, or *clan*, directly proceeded; and the
gens may be taken as the social basis of that
earliest society properly so called, whose economic
conditions are expressed in the phrase Primitive
Communism: the foundation of the gens-formation
primitive social organisation rested on. This formation, all but universal as it is, presents infinite variety
in points of detail in various peoples; but the main
characteristics are the same. The second great division
in the constitution of primitive society is the *tribe*.
The tribe consists in a group of families, clans, or
gentes, united together by some bond of consanguinity,
either real or supposed. The tribe and gens are the
component elements of the earliest organised society;
they may seldom be found in isolation, but they are
always distinguishable. Other and less important
divisions there are, † which vary according to time,
place, and circumstances, but these need not detain
us here. The dominating division primarily was
doubtless the gens. At a later period the influence
of the tribe gained the upper hand.

But new economical conditions, the introduction
of agriculture on a more extended scale, the taming
of domestic animals, the acquirement of extensive
property in flocks and herds and slaves (the cap-
tives taken in war), the beginnings of manufacture,
perhaps more than all, the improvement in weapons
of war, necessitating closer union and more systematic methods of offence and defence, led to a
new social formation, destined to overshadow the

* For a full description of this primitive form of the family, see
Morgan's "Ancient Society," also Engel's *Ursprung der Familie.*
† *E.g.*, the so-called *Phratric.*

original divisions of society. This was the consolidation, within a definite area under definite institutions, of an aggregate of tribes—in most cases previously knit together in a loose manner as a "people" by supposed ties of remote kinship —into a social system called the *city*. By the word "city" as here used must not be understood the material city or place of habitation, but rather the society which originated it, and of which the material city, with its buildings, etc., was the outward expression. The *city* was the turning-point in human development; in it we pass from barbarism —primitive society—to civilisation. The organisation of tribes into a more or less coherent "people" denotes the highest phase of primitive barbaric society (see Appendix, III.); the consolidation of the "people" into the organised "city" denotes the first stage in civilisation. (See Appendix, IV.) With the complete ascendency of the city, *quâ* city, over the earlier social forms within its pale, *society* has surrendered itself to the *state*. History—in the sense in which we use the word in the present article—has practically begun. But at the stage at which the city supersedes the gens and the tribe, a great change has already supervened in the primitive family organisation itself. The gens in its old form has fallen into abeyance, and the patriarchal family, with its despotic head, its wives, concubines, children, and slaves, which has sprung up out of it, now represents the unit of social life. Respecting the exact mode of the transformation of the gens-formation into the patriarchal family, we have but slight evidence; but it is nearly certain that from the first such authority or organising power as was necessary for the society was vested in the elders or fathers of the gens or tribe. This authority, as was natural, tended to grow and become re-

garded as sacred, together with the persons of its
possessors. Hence the beginnings of despotism.*

The ancient form of the gens survives in the
city, but it is mainly as a survival, and save for
its being the central point of some of the most
important religious sentiments and rites, tends to
lose more and more of its significance ; private
property, though not necessarily individual property,
has entered into the constitution of society. Classes
arise in addition to the fundamental class division
between slave and freeman,—classes *within* the
free population of the city. But sometimes the
city is not able to maintain an independent and
separate existence. In this case it is in its turn
absorbed into a larger unity, just as it had itself
already absorbed the family and the tribe. This
larger unity is the federation of cities (as it is
in its origin), which subsequently becomes conso-
lidated into the kingdom or empire,—such as
Egypt, Assyria, Babylonia, Phœnicia, China, or
India. The usual, although not invariable tendency
is, for the imperial bond, at first loose and purely
of the nature of a federal overlordship, to become
drawn closer and closer until the city-state has
in extreme cases become completely subordinated
to the imperial state.

Such is the general description of the stages
which, so far as we can see, led up to the vast
Oriental civilisations with which universal history
begins. In these, although more or less over-
shadowed and in abeyance, the earlier social forms
are distinctly present as elements in the constitution of society. There is a family organisation, a

* It is in the Semitic peoples that the patriarchal phase in the
evolution of the family is most strongly marked, and shows the
greatest tenacity of life. In the Aryan races it is in general much
less accentuated, and consequently tends to pass away much sooner.
The Romans, however, form a noteworthy exception in this respect.

tribal organisation, and a civic organisation, each
with a special cultus of its own, and each presided
over by its respective civil and religious head,
on the principle of a hierarchy. The fact of the
combination of sacerdotal and governmental functions in the same person shows us that religion
is not as yet separated from the life of the community; that it still means no more than the
ideal expression of social life; a devotion to the
social whole, and a care for all that contributes
to its maintenance and well-being. Nature is as
yet not formally separated from Man, nor the
individual from his social surroundings. The hearth
and its sacred fire remains the central embodiment
of the highest religious sentiment. The courts of
the temples and the sacred fanes themselves are
rendezvous for the business and pleasure of the
citizens. But the antagonism is developing itself,
and although not formally recognised, is everywhere present. A vast slave population has grown
up in subordination to the free, while the distinction between poor and rich grows ever more
marked. With the leisure and culture which accumulation of wealth affords, the old _naïve_ belief
in the unity of nature and man has become
weakened and modified. With industrial development a new division frequently obtains, based
not upon the old social principle of kinship, but
upon the economical one of occupation. Certain
families and tribes assume a particular order of
handicraft or other employment which becomes
hereditary, and to which they are fixed by custom
or law. Thus a warrior caste, a sacerdotal caste,
a manufacturing caste arises, the pre-eminent influence of the wealthy classes, composed of the more
ancient families, culminating in the civil, military,
and religious chief. All we know of the ancient

civilisations tends to show us that some such system as is here described prevailed in the earliest period of universal history,—in Egypt, Assyria, Babylonia, the Palestine of Solomon's days, etc. But though the material antagonism between individual and community, no less than the speculative antagonism between nature and spirit, has begun, yet, judged from the standpoint of to-day, it may well seem but little developed in these civilisations. It is probable that extreme poverty and starvation were unknown in them as class-conditions ; while, although private property-holding existed, the "absolute rights of property," in the modern sense of the word, were certainly unrecognised, since all property, in case of need, was at the disposal of the state. Religion, as we have already pointed out, concerned itself exclusively with the community, and with this world, and in no way with the individual and another world. The religions of antiquity, even when the earliest belief in the immediate personification of nature, was more or less on the wane, still conceived of man and nature as bound together by a system of subtle affinities, the knowledge of which was requisite to the well-being of the commonwealth, to the end that they might be regulated to its advantage. It was still the highest aspiration of the individual to found a family—that his life as part of the community should be immortal ; as to his own personality, his only care was to devote himself to the city, and when his course was done, to go down to his fathers in the under-world of shades. Such science as existed consisted in astrology and magic, in accordance with the prevalent conception of the universe. It was a branch of the state-organisation, which kept in view the importance of the priestly caste, which

in these early civilisations was the embodiment of
the highest existing culture. (See Appendix, V.)

The Oriental monarchies began to be superseded
about from the eighth to the sixth century B.C.
by the Greek races. In the Oriental monarchy
the city tended to become strangled by the empire.
When the free development of the city was once
arrested, the whole civilisation began to stagnate
or to crystallise into set forms. It then either
lingered on for a time, like Egypt, or became
the prey of free neighbouring peoples, like Assyria.
Once the East became stationary, and the *lead* in
human progress passed on to the peoples of South-
eastern Europe (first to the Greek commmunities
and their colonies, and afterwards to those of
Italy), where, owing to topographical and other
causes, the city-form had not been superseded
by the federal or imperial bond. It is, therefore,
in these Aryan peoples of South-eastern Europe
and in those of Asia Minor, that we meet with
the purest type of the ancient city. All we have
said hitherto respecting the city in its social and
religious aspect applies with especial force to the
classical city, more particularly in the earlier phases
of its development. In this second period of ancient history the development of antagonism goes
on apace, the mainspring of political development
—the city—being henceforth free. In the cities
of the classical world we have the most perfect
specimens of the prehistoric tribal and gental forms,
after they have been absorbed into the state.
Nothing is plainer in classical history than the
vitality of the old religious spirit. "The city,"
says Fustel de Coulanges, speaking of the classical
city, "was founded on religion and constituted like
a church. Hence its power; hence also its omni-
potence and the absolute empire it exercised over

its members. In a society established on such principles individual liberty could not exist. The citizen was subject in all things and without reserve to the city; he belonged to it entirely. The religion which had given birth to the city, and the city which regulated religion, were not two things, but one. These two powers, associated and inseparable, constituted an almost superhuman might, to which mind and body were alike subject." For a long time after the antagonism of interest between individual and community was strongly developed in the economic sphere, the great end of religion and morality still continued to be social. The introspective ethics of individualism were not from the first so congenial to the Aryan races, as they were to the Semitic.

In the cities of the classical world we have a wealth of material preserved, in which we may trace individual interest steadily gaining the upper hand over social interest; while at the same time the supernatural view of the universe and man's relation to it as steadily supersedes the old *naïve* and natural one. Here also, as in the Oriental world, a slave-holding production, of which direct exploitation of human labour-power was the special form, tended to supersede all free labour. This was now exercised for the benefit of the individual rich citizen, and not, as in earlier stages, for that of the gens, the tribe, or the city. The religion, again, notwithstanding the vigorous survival of its original forms, steadily gave way before the advance of individualism; it inevitably became less social and more personal. The various "mysteries" which sprang into vogue, many of them imported from the East, had for their end the setting forth of the mystical relation of the individual to the supposed divinity outside nature.

The gods themselves gradually became transported to a heaven above the nature and society of which previously they were simply the personifications. The ghosts of ancestors, too, became relegated to the same super-sensible sphere. But these tendencies cannot be said to have fully realised themselves until the city-form had been reduced to a meaningless phrase, had developed its own contradiction, in the great city-empire of Rome; although from the earliest period in which the Greek cities appear on the arena of history we can see them at work. As already stated, at first the classical city seems to embody considerable traces of the primitive communistic society out of which it arose; but as the Greek cities developed, productive labour came to be more and more relegated to the slave population, who far exceeded the limited number of freemen. Exchange of commodities— commerce—now took place on a much more extended scale than before,—a circumstance facilitated by the opening of the Egyptian ports. The internal struggle which characterised the growth of the Greek or Roman states between the rich minority and poor majority of free inhabitants of the city was the framework within which the principle of individualism in economics asserted itself in the ancient world. (See Appendix, VI.) It is important to understand the meaning of these struggles, which in their main features seem so uniform in character. Their meaning would seem to be this. The so-called democracies of the classical cities were really a middle class, in many cases composed largely of aliens, or at least persons belonging to none of the older gentes. In breaking down the ancient aristocracies they were really breaking down the social institutions which had descended from early society, but which in the course of time had lost

meaning, or redounded merely to the advantage
of a clique of privileged families. The strife between the aristocratic and democratic factions was
a struggle for political equality among the freemen. But on neither side was there any idea
of the great slave majority of the state having
any rights at all. The economic development
made the individual citizen's gain and advancement, whether as trader, mercenary soldier, or
professional politician, a point of first importance
in life. But even in spite of this the religious
bond of solidarity with the city-state sufficed to
prevent the complete ascendency of individual over
social interest (in the limited sense in which the
latter was then understood). The state had not
as yet entirely lost its social character; it had
not quite degenerated into a mere machine for
protecting property and privilege. Now just as
the material ascendency of individual interest was
undermining the old religious sentiment described,
there appeared on the market-place at Athens a
teacher, giving utterance to a doctrine which implied the undermining of it from its moral side.
In the "Know thyself" of Socrates we have the
first expression in the Greek world of that personal morality as opposed to the old social morality, which culminated in the Christianity of
later ages. The Athenians felt instinctively the
danger of this new ethic, and in a panic condemned Socrates to death for proclaiming it. (See
Appendix, VII.) But it had taken root already, and
the writings of Plato and Aristotle exhibit the two
moralities in conflict and an ineffectual attempt to
reconcile them. From this time forward the progressive weaning of the mind from its old conception
of nature, and its old satisfaction in the "city,"
becomes marked; although it was given to the

dreamy Semitic rather than to the practical Aryan intellect to be the typical exponent of the new tendency. The races of South-eastern Europe were destined in the ancient world to work out the opposition of interest between individual and society on its economical side; but for a satisfactory ethic of Individualism they had to look to Western Asia. This ethnical peculiarity is illustrated by the unsatisfactoriness of the Greek attempts in this direction, which, although making much noise with the educated, evoked but little enthusiasm even among their votaries, and none among ordinary men. We refer, of course, to the various philosophical sects—Cynic, Cyreniac, Stoic, Epicurean—which arose during the declining period of Greek independence. As the old political life of the Greek cities was dying out, the cultivated citizen turned his attention to the question of the most satisfactory manner in which he, as an individual, could spend his life. The "philosopher" and the "virtuous man," wrapped up in himself, superseded the "citizen" among the educated classes. The thoughtful man began to feel disgust at the old morality which was limited in its application to the single city-state, and did not apply to all the members of that. Yet he in vain searched for something satisfactory to supply its place.

Such was the Greek world when the victorious Roman armies destroyed the last vestige of Greek independence by reducing the country to a Roman province, from which event the "lead" in historical progress—i.e., in the development of the dual opposition between individual and society, and between nature and spirit—passed on to the new city-empire. In imperial Rome, as already observed, the ancient city-form evolved its own contradiction.

The moment the city became an imperial centre, owning nominal citizens among every people, its citizenship being reduced to a mere commercial value, from that time forward it is plain that the sacredness, the meaning, the reality of the ancient city-form had passed away. The last vestige of primitive society with the political exclusiveness it implied had given place to a cosmopolitanism in which social solidarity lingered solely as a survival in the official religion, and in which in reality individual interest alone obtained. Historically the function of the Roman empire answers in the political sphere to the function of Christianity in the religious sphere, namely, the destruction of the tribal and race exclusiveness, which had had its day. (See Appendix, VIII.) This meant on its obverse side absolute predominance of the individual—i.e., of individual interest—in the one case in economics, in the other in ethics and religion.

The earlier historical development of the Roman city does not differ essentially from that of the Greek cities; but our information is fuller in the one case than in the other. We can trace the development of oppositions more in detail in Roman history. Rome is the type of the later classical evolution. As soon as all public offices were thrown open to the Plebeian, all public life became a scramble for wealth. The antagonism between private and common interest, or, which is the same thing, between individual and community, manifested itself here, as elsewhere, in the degeneration of the gentes which had originally formed the whole city into a privileged aristocratic *class* within the city. This naturally brought in its train the opposition of all elements of later date. The struggle of these elements for equality meant the breaking-down of the now obsolete survivals

of the ancient communal and tribal system, and
its complete reconstruction on the basis of wealth
and individual property. For these opposing classes
(the Plebs) it must be remembered had little or
no tribal solidarity among themselves. They were
composed largely of heterogeneous elements, the
only bond of cohesion between them being the
city within whose domains they dwelt, and for
which they fought, but from the inner civil and
religious system of which they were for a long
time excluded, and which in consequence it was
their aim to deprive as far as possible of its
meaning. The Plebs, at first, largely consisted of
small farmers and poor handicraftsmen who worked
for their living; but with the development of the
State politically and economically, with the great
slave imports derived from foreign conquest, etc.,
a wealthy commercial Plebs arose, and it was this
Plebs that profited by the reforms in the constitution, while in the same proportion the poorer
Plebs became less and less able to cope with the
slave-holding production now becoming universal.
This poorer class of freemen must, indeed, have
succumbed altogether, or else have created a social
revolution, had it not been for the fact that to
the last so much primitive communism remained
in the Roman state-system that no free citizen
could starve, since he could always obtain sufficient for his maintenance from public resources.
With the conquest of Greece, B.C. 146, Rome
inherited the more advanced culture of the Greek
world. By this means progress in civilisation—or,
which is the same thing, progress in corruption—
was enormously accelerated. The Gracchan legislation marks the period of the complete ascendency
of Roman Bourgeoisdom as such. From this time
forward the power of the money-bag was supreme.

The imperial policy itself no longer had for its object the glory of the city, but simply and solely the conquest of new provinces for the sake of the aggrandisement either by direct plunder or by oppressive taxation, of the particular party which happened to be in power in Rome, together with its enormous army of dependents.

In morality and religion the same symptoms we have already noticed as belonging to the decline of Greek independence appear in an intensified form—*i.e.*, the withdrawal of culture and intelligence from public affairs, and their concentration on the individual and the problem of his happiness. All the Greek sects, claiming to offer a solution of this now all-important problem, spread rapidly. These, to a large extent, sought the conditions of happiness in this life. But there was another and deeper phase of the same movement which was characterised by a contempt for nature, society, and this world, and a concentration on the notion of another life beyond the grave. This craving was sought to be satisfied by the introduction of new mystical Oriental cults, and in various other ways. To be brief, these symptoms of the divorce of the individual from the life of the state, and his concentration on himself, together with those of the rise of a speculative dualism between nature and spirit, alike found their ultimate idealistic expression in the great Semitic creed—Christianity, —the religion of individual salvation and of the other world. The accentuation of the practical antagonism between individual and community, between private and public interest, and of the speculative antagonism between nature and spirit, between this world and the other world, went on apace as the twilight of ancient civilisation gradually deepened into darkness.

The outward shell of the forms of ancient city
life, rotten through and through, was shattered in
the fifth and sixth centuries by the German tribes,
fresh from their primitive village communities. In
the establishment of Christianity, personal as opposed to social morality and the religion of another
world, as opposed to the ancient social religions of
this world, had first received official expression. The
Christian empire accordingly presented both economically and ethically a more complete triumph of
the principle of individualism over the principle of
socialism than the world had seen before. The
opposition between the various phases of human
life was becoming concentrated in the great antithesis of the Middle Ages between religious and
secular. The Græco-Roman world steadily pro-
gressed from its earlier communistic form, in which
the city was all in all towards the ascendency of
individual interest here and hereafter; and the
progress culminated in its death as a civilisation.
But the economic forms of which civilisation is
capable had as yet not all been passed through.
The classical development was limited in various
ways; first it was limited ethnically, it centred
itself in one particular branch of the Aryan race,
the Græco-Roman, and left entirely out of account
another equally important branch, the Teutonic;
secondly, it was limited economically by the conditions of a slave-holding production. This is
essentially different from our modern capitalistic
production. Men had as yet imperfectly learnt
the art of buying in order to sell again; the
middleman was absent. The wealthy Roman purchased what slave handicraftsmen and labourers
he could, and enriched himself directly by their
labour. The element of exchange value *per se*,
which rules to-day with a rod of iron, entered

in a very minor degree into the constitution of classical society. Trade would seem to have been viewed by the classic much as card-sharping is by us. Thus Cicero, in his "De Officiis," speaks of trade as disreputable, while Suetonius says of the Emperor Vespasian: "He likewise engaged in a pursuit disgraceful even in a private individual, buying great quantities of goods, for the purpose of selling them again to advantage." It is obvious, therefore, that the great economic expression of an individualistic society—viz., commerce—had very imperfectly established itself in the classical world. It was not until humanity had passed through another distinct period of development,— a period in which the Teutonic races were the chief actors,—that the opposition between individual and society attained the completeness towards which it tended.

The German tribes of the time of the Roman Empire, already constituted as "peoples," being in the highest phase of barbarism, and on the verge of civilisation, were (since the germ of a new society was already present in them) the fittest instruments for the transformation of the effete civilisation of antiquity into a new world. The German, fresh from his nature worship and his tribal communities, was precipitated headlong into a civilisation with its antagonisms fully developed— that is, as fully developed as was compatible with the then current economic conditions. The great industry being non-existent, the then world market having collapsed from various obvious causes, the old slave production became unprofitable. Vast numbers of slaves were, therefore, virtuously and religiously manumitted, in order to save the expense of their maintenance. "Slavery," says Engels, "ceased to pay, and, therefore, it died out. But

it left its sting behind it in the freeman's contempt for productive labour. . . . Slavery was economically impossible, the labour of freemen was
morally despised. The one had ceased to be, the
other had not begun to be the ground-form of
social production. The only help here was a complete revolution." And, in fact, an economic as
well as a racial revolution did take place. The
feudal system, which was the ultimate issue of
this revolution, was nothing else than primitive
communistic society, with the notion of sovereignty
on the part of the head of the community super-
added. It is true, this was a modification of the
first importance, but it must not be forgotten that
it was limited in many ways, and that it did not
prevent the serf of the Middle Ages from being,
as a rule, in a far better condition than the slave
of antiquity, not to speak of the modern labourer.

Religion had in the mediæval period a twofold
aspect. On the one side was the Church hierarchy,
the legacy of the Roman Empire, on the model
of whose organisation it was formed. This, with
its elaborate body of semi-pagan ceremonials, customs, and rites, entered closely into the whole
political and social constitution of the Middle Ages.
As a political power it claimed supreme jurisdiction
over emperors and kings. Its superior clergy and
religious corporations were themselves powerful
feudal potentates, possessing vast territories with
all the rights of independent sovereigns. As a
social power its influence, its rites, ceremonies
and superstitions, entered into all relations in life
It gave a religious colouring to every department
of human interests. Even the merchant guilds,
and after them the craft guilds, were in a sense
religious bodies,—a fact which served Henry VIII.
with a plausible excuse for confiscating their pro-

perty under the edict abolishing the religious orders. Side by side with this aspect of religion in which it simply ideally expressed the general social and political life of the community much in the same way as the religions of antiquity, was its essentially Christian aspect, that of a personal, introspective, and spiritualistic theory of the universe and of life. This more distinctively Christian side of Catholicism, although never dominant during the Middle Ages, was continually manifesting itself in a sporadic manner; its most remarkable products being Francis of Assissi and Thomas à Kempis. It influenced in some cases those who sought refuge from the world in the monasteries and various religious brotherhoods that arose, having personal holiness and salvation as their aim. But it never entered into the ordinary everyday life of the average man and woman, as was subsequently the case with Protestantism. The barbarians had accepted Christianity; they accepted, that is, a religion which in its inner significance belonged to a period of ultra-civilisation, which was the supreme expression of the revolt of the individual against the old social morality and against the old conception of the universe ; in short, which presupposed a long development. Much of the old tribal morality of the Germans, and many of their old modes of thought continued, therefore, to exist under the sanction of the Church, and to this we owe the chivalry and "honour" of the Middle Ages, besides much of their folk-lore and superstition. Add to this that the Church itself, modelled as it was externally on the Roman imperial system, had absorbed, with but little modification, large fragments of classical paganism. But, as we have said, the individualism and supernaturalism of Christianity subsisted side by side with the semi-paganism of the popular creed. It was always the ultimate court of appeal, and supplied what was considered as the highest object in life—namely, preparation for another world. The poetry, the chivalry, the enthusiasm of the Middle Ages are clearly traceable to their barbaric side, and in no wise to the creed of the *blasé* Roman world. (See Appendix, IX.) The mediæval mind had reserved to itself the idea of two separate spheres,— a religious and a secular. To the "secular" man religion consisted in external and pagan observances, in consideration of which the Church guaranteed his ultimate salvation. It was only to the monastic recluse, and rarely even to him, that religion was a personal matter. Not until the final disruption of the mediæval system and the ascendency of the middle class Protestant creed, did the theory of individual freedom of contract here and hereafter come into general vogue. The Church, in spreading its glamour over every department of human life, from war to handicraftship, which thus came to have a mystical religious significance attaching to them, was only fulfilling the function and acting as the succedaneum of the old family, tribal, and social religion of the heathen German, in which the opposition between sacred and profane did not exist. The mediæval instinct with true logicality felt that it was needful for the man who aspired to the truly and specially Christian ideal of personal holiness to come out of a world in which the personality merely counted as part of the general social hierarchy.

We may divide the Middle Ages into two epochs. The first, the period of Feudalism proper, that is, of production on a small scale for use on the feudal estate, in which exchange was very limited. This period we may roughly assign to from the

eighth to the thirteenth century. Towards its close
a surplus began to be produced for purposes of
commerce. Markets for the exchange of necessaries
and luxuries became more numerous. Finally, independent townships arose, that is, the villeins
clustered together on the larger estates, especially
the ecclesiastical, shook off the more onerous feudal
dues in consideration of an annual rental, while
within these towns a distinct industrial system
arose under the auspices of the guilds. This brings
us to the second period of the Middle Ages, which
may also be approximately assigned to from the
thirteenth to the sixteenth century. This is the
flourishing age of the guild industry, and during
this period arose the first form of the opposition
between middle class and proletariat. The guilds
naturally soon developed into close corporations,
entry to which became hedged round with ever-
increasing expenses and difficulties. For all that
the great social struggle of the period was between
the burghers and the nobles. The typical instance
of this struggle is the revolt in the Netherlands
under the Arteveldtes against the Count of Flanders.
The gradually lapsing power of feudalism proper
was shown in the comparative freedom the agricultural serf had acquired, and the attempt to
deprive him of which in England was the main
cause of the Wat Tyler insurrection. This interesting and important period to be properly dealt
with demands a separate treatise.

In the sixteenth century the antagonism latent in
mediæval society had reached a point of development
which was incompatible with the continued existence
of that society. The world-market was opening up.
The middle classes had become one of the most important factors in civilisation. The modern national
systems of Europe were becoming fixed. Trade and

industry were everywhere in the ascendant. Besides this, the Christian religion was emerging from the semi-pagan form it had assumed during the Middle Ages, and asserting in their fulness the individualist and introspective tendencies peculiar to it. The distinction between religious and secular was only broken down on one side to reappear with increased asperity on another. Protestantism proclaimed the doctrine of *personal* salvation by faith alone—*i.e.*, the whole of religion was resolved into a purely personal matter, with reference to which, as extreme Protestant sects like the Puritans very logically maintained, a Church tradition and organisation were entirely superfluous. In Protestantism the supremacy of individualism in religion, its antagonism to the old social religions, reaches its highest point of development. It has shaken off the last fragment of pagan poetry and sentiment, if not of pagan doctrine. It is personal and matter of fact. Under Protestantism religion has become necessarily divorced from worldly avocations. The continual interruption to industry, the time allowed by Catholicism in its festivals and holidays for enjoyment, not less than the time exacted for penance, etc., could not be tolerated. The rising middle classes were beginning to find out the "dignity of labour," that it was appointed to men to work, etc., and that the longer the journeyman worked, and the less time he wasted in amusement, the better it was for his soul and their bodies.

History from the sixteenth century downwards is a picture of the struggle of the rising middle or manufacturing and trading classes, to emancipate themselves from the trammels of the feudal or landowning classes, and thereby to attain to individual freedom of action in the furthering of private

interests.   Of the causes, such as the dissolution
of the old feudal estates, the appropriation of
common lands, the new inventions, etc., which all
contributed to bring about the rise of capitalism
as the leading economical form of society, it is
unnecessary to say anything in this place ; our
purpose here being, to suggest the ultimate meaning of universal history from the point of view
of modern socialism, rather than to expound the
modus operandi of historic evolution.   There is
one fact, however, to be noted which is extremely
significant, namely, that the ascendency of the
middle classes in the shape they now assumed
was incompatible with the continued existence of
the old guild organisations.   The guilds had the
reason of their being in feudal privilege and landed
tenure like the nobles ; like the latter the power
of these great municipal monopolies began rapidly
and hopelessly to decline in proportion to the
strides made by the new individualist capitalism.
The middle class of the second mediæval period
(as we have termed it) was essentially an aristocracy.   The mediæval city of the fifteenth century was in some respects a kind of rude reflex
of the classical city ; if we like to carry out the
parallel, we may compare the guildsmen to the
patricians, the journeymen to the plebeians, and
the apprentices, who were *in statu pupillari*, and,
therefore, without rights at all, to the slave class.
The new capitalistic middle class differed from the
guildsmen of old as the new proletariat, the pre-
cursor of the proletariat of to-day, differed from
the merry journeymen of the mediæval township.

But the meaning of history since the close of
the mediæval period is so plain as to be unmis-
takable.   Every political aspiration, every political
reform, has meant a breaking asunder of the bonds

which held the old civilisation together, the freeing
of the individual from the duties now obsolete
which bound him in some sort to the social whole.
In Economics the middle-class revolution accomplished itself immediately through the subdivision
of labour and the workshop system, the so-called
periode manufacturière, in the course of which
the master gradually ceased to be himself a worker,
and became an overseer. The gradual and apparently limitless unfolding of the world-market
assisted the development, but its final phase was
reached in the great machine industry which from
the last quarter of the eighteenth century to our
own day has been steadily progressing.

In Politics the movement was characterised by
the consolidation of the European nationalities (in
the Middle Ages loose feudal confederacies), which
was accomplished by (1) bureaucratic centralisa-
tion; (2) the extension of royal prerogative; and
(3) the rise of modern commercial patriotism. Its
great political expression is Constitutionalism—*i.e.*,
the real supremacy of the middle classes in the
State, though this may in some cases be varnished
over by the nominal ascendancy of the older order,
as in England. This was finally and definitely
attained by the French Revolution of 1789.

In Religion it is expressed in the accentuation
of the Protestant doctrine before alluded to, of
" the religion of the heart," that is, of the working
out of your own salvation, as opposed to the
mediæval Catholic doctrine, that belonging to the
Church organisation itself constitutes a claim to
the Kingdom of Heaven. This is a theme upon
which the evangelical preacher is never tired of
enlarging. It is also shown in the separation of
religion from daily life, as expressed in the emphasis laid upon the distinction between sacred and

profane ; in short, in the modern Protestant notion
of *reverence*. (See Appendix, X.) To the mediæval
mind, trinity, saints, and angels were little more than
a company of boon companions, whose adventures
could be represented on the stage of any village fair
with edification to the beholder. The miracle-plays
extant (which it must be remembered were played
often by priests themselves, and always under the
auspices of the Church) contain what the modern
Protestant mind would deem blasphemies, compared
to which those of Mr. George Foote are reverential.
The notion of "reverence," like that of personal
religion, is the creation of that middle-class order
which took its first rise in the sixteenth, and has
culminated in the world of the nineteenth century.

In its Morality the individualistic character of
the movement is no less apparent than in its
religion. Bourgeois morality is eminently personal.
A man in his public acts, in all he does that
concerns the people, may prove himself an ill-con-
ditioned ruffian or an unscrupulous adventurer,
careless though he plunge a whole nation into
misery to serve his own purposes or ambition; he
may be a Napoleon III., a Prince Imperial, a
Bartle Frere, a Gordon ; yet he may still, if he
only make himself sufficiently prominent, expect
honourable mention when living and a public
monument when dead. All is fair it is said in
love and war. This principle is nowadays extended
to public life generally, and in politics all is fair
that tends to personal advancement. The man
who takes a serious view of social and political
duty is an enthusiast or a fool to be laughed at.
Not so he who can persuade the public, whether
truly or not, that he is that rather washed-out
product of the nineteenth century, the "man without a vice." This man extolled for the "purity"

of his life may commit any public rascality he
pleases ; on the other hand, if an offence against
the conventional personal ethics were brought home
to a man, it would be deemed sufficient to blast
the most single-minded public career.

And what does this middle-class order mean with
its isolation of every aspect or department of human
life from every other ? The only answer that can
be given on the lines of the foregoing argument
is that it denotes the final phase of Civilisation.
Here the antitheses, latent in primitive human
society, for the first time reach their fullest development. The cardinal practical antagonism (as
we have termed it) between individual and community has resulted in the complete subjection of
social or public, to individual or private interest.
Ever since civilisation began, the aim of man has
been to free himself as individual from what he
conceived to be his bondage to the social whole.
The moment he distinguished his private interest
or property from the public interest or property
of the society of which he was part, from that
moment did history begin in its long array of
crimes, tyrannies, and slaughters. An economic and
social individualism necessarily implied sooner or
later a change in the conception of duty. With
the abstraction of individual interest from its relation to the common interest of society came that
other abstraction expressed in the great speculative
antagonism between Nature and Spirit, World and
God, Body and Soul, etc. This speculative antagonism has reacted on the practical ; it has
superseded the old ethical sentiment by placing
the individual man's highest object of duty and
devotion, not in the society without him, but in
the Divinity believed to be revealed within him ;
by placing the goal of human aspiration, not in

this world, but in another world; by lulling individuals and classes into condoning their sufferings
here by holding out imaginary hopes of bliss
hereafter. Thus has the natural been completely
subjugated by the spiritual in the popular theology
and ethics.

The principles here indicated were nearly, although not quite (for reasons before stated), realised
in the decadent period of the Roman Empire.
Now, at last, they are present in their rankest
growth, and constitute the essence of our nine-
teenth-century world. Along a steep and tortuous
path man has attained to a complete civilisation.
Above the gods, said the Greeks, are the fates;
and a strange fate it is which has lured, nay,
forced, man forward by the very necessities of
his existence, under the pretence of realising his
liberty as an individual, to such a shrine as this.
Now, in a sense, the goal of the march of history
is attained, attained in the victory of principles
which are the antithesis of those under the auspices
of which civilisation started, but whose ultimate
realisation civilisation implied. In the well-known
phrase, "Every man for himself, and God for us
all," or in that other phrase, which is, indeed, the
same thing otherwise expressed, "The devil take
the hindmost," we have a rough and concise statement of that principle of individualism and of the
relegation of religion to a supersensible sphere,
which together form the pillars of the modern
world.

But have these principles, for which so many
in days gone by have fought and bled, have
they realised the happiness expected of them?
Here they are; you have it now all for which
you have craved. And what has it proved? Now
that the fruit of individualism is plucked; by the

virtual admission of every thinking person, whether
socialist or not, it is but Dead Sea fruit after
all. In the supremacy of individual interest here
and hereafter was seen the mirage of human happiness and progress. Once attained, and behold
the fancied happiness is an illusion; hence that
characteristic product of the present day—cynical
pessimism. The ordinary mind sees the illusion,
but cannot see beyond it—cannot see that the
mirage which has lured men on, although in itself
a phantasm, is yet the foretaste of a reality more
distant, yet none the less real for that; and that
the dreary waste which the place of the mirage
proved to be, had to be traversed before the reality
lying below its horizon could be reached.

In the present day the abstract, the nominal
freedom of the individual is complete. But individualism has no sooner shaken itself free from
the supports which, though they may have cum-
bered it in its advance, yet did at least keep it
from falling; it has no sooner completely realised
itself, than its death-knell is rung, and it finds
itself strangled by the very economical revolution
which had rendered its existence possible. For
that revolution which has brought about an absolute separation of classes, has deprived the one
class of all individuality whatever, albeit their
abstract freedom still remains to mock them. Production in its process has become more than ever
before social and co-operative, notwithstanding that
its end and object is more than ever before mere
individual aggrandisement. The majority are the
slaves of modern Industrialism. Individualism,
therefore, for the majority has become a meaningless phrase. The same with supernatural religion.
The distinction between God and World has practically ceased to exist for the educated classes.

With the Hegelian philosophy and that vast body of contemporary thought which, whether consciously or unconsciously, is the outcome of that philosophy, the distinction survives merely as a conventional phrase.

What, then, does all this point to, if it does not point to the fact that civilisation, having accomplished its end in social evolution, must cease to be; that it must suffer a transformation, in the course of which its essential nature will be abolished? Its essential nature, as we have sought to show, consists in antagonism—antagonism of class, creed, nationality. *It involves an isolation or abstraction of every aspect of human life from every other;* it is the direct negation of the communistic solidarity in which the nature of pre-historic society consisted, and in which politics, morality, religion, and art were as yet undivided from each other, and from the life of the whole. Now, civilisation, we have said, is the negation of this primitive society as implying universal division, strife, and opposition. But if the next stage in evolution implies the negation of the opposition of which civilisation consists, it must mean a return in a sense to the conditions of primitive society. Two negations make an affirmation. The negation of civilisation, which is itself the negation of early society, must, therefore, mean a return to the essential characteristic of that society—*i.e.*, Solidarity, Communism, or Socialism. We say the essential characteristic, as, of course, although the socialistic world of the future will present a correspondence with the socialised world of the past, it will be a correspondence on a higher plane—a likeness in difference. The passage from Primitive Communism to the Communism of the future was only possible through the mediation of History otherwise expressed, of Individualism. It was impossible for the race solidarity, on which early society was based, and which is implied in its economies, in its ethics, in its religion, and its art, to pass at once into that human solidarity for which we are preparing to-day. The race barrier had to be broken down, effectually and completely, and this could only be done by the temporary sacrifice of the social principle itself. The early solidarity of kinship had to be resolved into its direct antithesis —individualism, universal and world-wide. Individualism in economics, in ethics, in religion, was the necessary intermediate step before the final goal of universal solidarity or communism, which unites the solidarity of early society with the cosmopolitan principle of individualism, could be reached. The society of the future will not be limited by consideration of kinship or of frontier, as was the society of the past. It will embrace the whole world, irrespective of race, in so far as it has overcome civilisation and become socialised. The test will be one of principle, not of blood. The infirmities of early society, its spirit of race exclusiveness, with its unconsciousness of the meaning of the changes it underwent, its ignorance of nature, its crudity of conception,—these things have passed away for ever. Yet none the less will the society of the future, to which socialists look forward, be a society in which all interests are again united, since they will all have a definite social aim ; in other words, since the interest of the individual will be once more identified, and this time *consciously*, with the interest of the community ; and lastly, since our ideal will cease to have for its object God and "another world," and be brought back to its original sphere of social life and "this world."

How or when this great revolution will take place we are not now concerned to discuss; whether, as some think, the Slav races of the East will be the chief actors in it, or whether it will be carried out by the older Western nations. To the present writer there seems a kind of solemnity in the drama of universal history—of humanity overcome and crucified by the wealth and organisation which is the work of its own hand. It is only relieved by the thought that the old Pagan-Christian myth of purification through suffering is susceptible of a new application here. Mankind having passed through the fire of the state-world, of Civilisation, of history, must come out the stronger and more perfect. Latterday society redeemed from Civilisation will be a higher and a more enduring society than that early society which knew no Civilisation. It is towards this world, where Civilisation shall have ceased to be, that the socialist of to-day casts his eyes. In this he has a right to feel that in a literal sense his faith and his hope is founded on the "rock of ages;" that where the ages are for him, nought can be against him.

"There amidst the world new builded shall our earthly deeds abide,
Though our names be all forgotten, and the tale of how we died."

A FRENCH ECONOMIST ON COLLECTIVISM.*

SOME one (Macaulay I think) said that a new doctrine passed through three stages, that of ridicule, argument, and acceptance. The new economy must have certainly reached the second of these stages, to judge by the flood of literature, which pretends to be serious in combating the theory of Scientific Socialism, that is pouring from the press both English and foreign. Whether the traditional economists will reach the third stage ere the shadow of death overtakes them and the society they represent is doubtful. There is one virtue conspicuously absent in English writers on the same side, which strikes one at the first glance in M. Leroy-Beaulieu's new work. He has certainly read what he is professing to criticise, but beyond this our praise for his fairness can hardly extend. His book is from beginning to end a tissue of cases of verbal quibble, of *ignoratio elenchi,* and here and there even of what looks like wilful misrepresentation. We do not know whether it is the moral or the intellectual side of M. Leroy-Beaulieu's character that is to blame for these things, but there they are.

* "Le Collectivisme. Examen Critique du Nouveau Socialisme," par Paul Leroy-Beaulieu, Membre de l'Institut, etc. Paris : Guillemin et Cie.

In an introductory chapter the author sketches the progress of Socialism within the last few years. He here endeavours to fix the terms—Socialist, Collectivist, Communist. The first he justly regards as generic, covering a variety of views more or less divergent. But the retention of the term Communism for the crude Utopic conception of the direct, equal, and periodical division of the objects of consumption involves an ignoring of the more recent history of the word, which is surely, to say the least, injudicious. However, if we once grant M. Leroy-Beaulieu his definitions, we must admit that he adheres to them with tolerable consistency throughout. A general and somewhat discursive criticism follows (embracing Henry George, Laveleye, Marx, Schäffle, etc.) of the charges brought by Socialist and semi-Socialist writers against the current economic *régime*. This includes some chapters on primitive Communism, types of which are found in the Russian *Mir* and the Javan village community. The first division of the book terminates with a somewhat rambling homily on the terrible results likely to ensue from land-nationalisation. The second part is devoted to a more systematic attempt at criticism of the theoretic portions of Marx and Schäffle. (By-the-bye, why does M. Leroy-Beaulieu exclude the writings of Frederic Engels from his animadversions?)

In an ordinary magazine review it is obviously impossible to touch upon all the points raised in a work such as the present. We are, therefore, forced to confine ourselves to a few typical instances of M. Leroy-Beaulieu's mode of treatment. An attempt is made at starting to confound sundry definitions established among Socialists. The method of obliterating real distinctions by verbal jugglery, and thus apparently landing an opponent in a *reductio ad absurdum*, is a specious one, and, as is well known, a favourite with sophists. By taking a conception in its most abstract

sense, carefully emptying it of all specific content, it
is easy enough to make everything nothing, and nothing everything.   It is this which Hegel means when
he declares the identity of Being and non-Being.   The
pure abstract form of any conception can be turned
inside out or outside in without making any difference.   Thus the wily Unionist posed the honest Home-
Ruler, who was pleading for his cause on the ground
of the right of peoples to self-government, by con-
tending that if Ireland were justified in detaching
herself from the United Kingdom, so, on like grounds,
would be any English county, town, or even any group
of persons inhabiting a particular plot of land, and
that *ergo* the right of Ireland to self-government was
illusory.   Now M. Leroy-Beaulieu tries this dialectical
trick on ; but he is not altogether successful in the
performance.   A little more practice is wanted.   For
instance, in seeking (page 17) to prove the fallacy of
the distinction between *bourgeois* and *proletaire*, he
asks whether the well-salaried manager of a wealthy
company, or the captain of a large vessel, etc., inasmuch as these cannot be said to possess the instruments
with which they work, are therefore to be ranked as
proletaires ; adding that if so, nine-tenths of those the
Socialists disdainfully term *bourgeois* are *proletaires.*
The answer to this is obvious, viz., that these middle-
men are placed in a *position of advantage* with reference to the instruments of production which practically
amounts *pro tanto* to possession.   This position of
advantage may arise from social connections, exceptional ability, or other things, but any way it lifts them
out of the arena of the labour market, and gives them
a control (more or less) over the means of production,
which the *proletaire* has not.   Again, M. Leroy-
Beaulieu sneeringly complains that, under a Collectivist *régime,* no one would be allowed to mend his
neighbour's trousers or shirt for a monetary considera-

tion, inasmuch as he would be then employing his
needle and thread for purposes of production, which
would be a return to Individualism, and hence illegal.
Let M. Leroy-Beaulieu reassure himself. All those
who desire to make a living by an individualistic
mending of shirts and trousers will be allowed full
liberty to satisfy their aspirations so far as any juridi-
cal coercion is concerned. We will not vouch for their
being much patronised, for the probability of repairs
of this character being executed better, more rapidly,
and with less expenditure of labour in the communal
workshop is great. But, in any case, they would have
their economic liberty to fatten on.

We find the assumption running through the whole
of M. Leroy-Beaulieu's book that the Collectivist in-
tends to suppress private production and exchange by
prohibitory laws. This is a crucial instance of his
want of grasp of the subject. Is it by prohibitory
laws that the *grande industrie* has supplanted the
petite industrie in well-nigh every branch of production? Prohibitory laws will be quite unnecessary
when private enterprise ceases to be profitable, as it
must when the whole of the means of production,
distribution, and credit, on a large scale, are in the
possession of the people themselves. References to
primitive communism, whether as established in the
Russian *Mir*, the Javan village, or the ancient German
commune, are obviously quite pointless as arguments
in discussing the organisation of the future, for the
simple reason that they belong to an anterior moment
of social evolution. Primitive *undifferentiated* Communism develops its own contradiction; a progress to
some form of Individualism is inevitable; this again
in its turn discovers within itself the germs of destruction. In the very act of realising its fullest and most
complete life, its doom is sealed. The individual
ceases to be producer, although possessing full control

over the exchange of the commodities produced. The
next step in progress is the *differentiated* Communism
or Collectivism, which with the production already
more than half-way socialised, completes the process,
and gives to the community a control over the exchange of that which is its collective product.*

To confute the Collectivist by proving what he never
doubts, namely, the tendency of primitive Communism
to issue in Individualism, is surely an *ignoratio elenchi*
of the baldest kind. Yet an important portion of
M. Leroy-Beaulieu's criticism is based thereon. "*Faut-*

---

* The above, of course, is an exposition in the abstract of the law
of economic development. In the absence of other factors every
society and, *à fortiori*, the history of the world would follow precisely this course, just as in the absence of all resistance motion
would pursue a straight line to infinity. But, as a matter of fact, in
the concrete there are other elements present which may retard,
accelerate, or modify, this process at any particular stage. Ethical,
religious, and political forms react upon the economical. Thus in
the earliest civilisations of the world we find the religious element
in the society dominating the whole; a hierarchy overlays the
original basis, which, while modifying it, preserves it from dissolution.
In the classical period a partial individualism obtains in economics
but is not yet officially reflected in religion. In the period of the
later Roman Empire, Individualism obtains in ethics and religion,
but the political hierarchy remains, and its forms are assimilated by
the new ecclesiasticism (partly as a necessity of its existence). A
new element now supervenes. The Germanic barbarians in full
"village community" pour in. The Roman imperial order, and the
hierarchy of the Church, the forms of both of which are indirectly
traceable to the organisation of the early theocratic monarchies, are
now met by simple primitive communism, Christian individualism
remaining, in theory at least, the ethical basis of society. The
fusion of these principles had as its result Catholic-feudal Europe.
Now, a complete Collectivism of society can never arise except out of
one in which individualism is completely worn out, *i.e.*, in which it
has completely prevailed, not merely in economics, but in politics,
religion, and ethics. In our modern society, for the first time in
the world's history, this condition is realised. Individualist anarchy
dominates every department of human life. In the sixteenth century the mediæval hierarchy was virtually broken up. From that
time forward individualism has steadily extended its sway, and now
reigns supreme. Hence it is that now, for the first time in the
world's history, a Collectivist reconstruction becomes possible.

il recommencer," says M. Leroy-Beaulieu (p. 150), " *une expérience déja faite pendant de longs siècles et qui a échoué partout."* The truth is, of course, that the experience has never been made, and never could have been made, till now. Our author evidently regards progress as linear. A very little acquaintance with the course of historic development would have sufficed to show him that (if we may employ metaphor in the matter) it is rather spiral, that is, that the same fact invariably returns in a higher form—in short, that the straight-line theory is a fallacy. Even Mr. Herbert Spencer recognises this in a manner. And if it be recognised, what becomes of the argument that, because one form of collective ownership was the economic beginning of social evolution, that, therefore, another form cannot be regarded as the end (see p. 148, *et seq.*).

We must confess to being surprised at the apparent inability of a Professor of Political Economy at the Collège de France to grasp the distinction between mere production *per se* and capitalistic production. We are told that Robinson in his island would have had capital if he had given himself the trouble to construct a wheelbarrow, since everything is capital that tends to increase the productivity of human labour. This again is either crass ignorance or a mere quibble about words, and does not really upset existent distinctions. It is quite clear that a radical difference exists between production for the sake of using the product, and production for the sake of effecting a gain on the exchange of the product. It is this latter kind of production that Marx understands, in accordance with current usage, as *capitalistic production.* To say that our ancestors of the stone age possessed capital in so far as they had flint implements wherewith to fashion their spear-heads, and that the distinction between these and the locomotive is only one of degree is obviously to evade the question. M. Leroy-Beaulieu may define capital in whatever eccentric way he likes, but in common fairness let him not blame Marx for not using the word according to his definition.

On page 254, M. Leroy-Beaulieu allows the cloven hoof to come out which proves him to be in hopeless confusion as to the dialectical method on which the whole of the critical portion of the *Kapital* is based. Marx describes money " as the final product of the circulation of commodities," adding, " This final product of the circulation of commodities is the first form of the appearance of Capital." This our eminent critic declares " inexact," in the first place, because " Capital," according to the Leroy-Beaulieu definition be it remembered (which the prophetic spirit of Marx doubtless ought to have foreseen), can exist apart from money. (Our author had previously declared it possible to exist apart from exchange altogether, so that its existence apart from money must under these circumstances *va sans dire.*) We then read, " *Dans bien des sociétés l'usage de l'or et de l'argent dans les échanges est rélativement nouveau, au moins comme fait universel.*" Precisely ; and this only proves that the principle enunciated by Marx is true, no less historically than it is logically. The exactitude of Marx's proposition was never more concisely admitted.

The truth of the thesis that capital everywhere presents itself historically in opposition to *land,* as *money* in one or other of its forms, is conceded, but pronounced to have hardly any importance from an economical point of view. We are not surprised that it should have little significance in the eyes of the author of the present volume, although, as a matter of fact, it gives us the philosophic key to the whole economic problem. *Land* is necessarily opposed to *money,* inasmuch as they are separated by the whole universe of commodities. They are logically antithetical by a whole series of momenta. At the one extreme of the process is *Land*, as the *formless Matter* of the economic world, at the other *Money*, as its *matterless Form*. *Land* is the *infinite possibility* of all economic things, as yet undetermined to anything in particular. *Money*, on the other hand, is the *indefinite actuality* of all such things, their determination as exchange-value. Between these two economically unreal extremes lies the real world of commodities for use, brought into being by the action of human labour on land or its natural products. *Labour* determines *land* or its products, gives it a specific and an individual form, in the commodity. The issue of the series of specific forms, ascending in complexity, is the money or pure form, which, although possessing no specific content in itself, is the abstract expression for the whole world of commodities which have led up to it. This abstraction, like "Almighty God" according to Scotus Erigena, may best be defined as "pure nothing" from the *real, i.e.*, the "utility" point of view. But as a matter of fact the economists like the theologians, have given their "pure-nothing" a local habitation and a name. *Its* name, too, is "Wonderful," "Counsellor," "Mighty God" (of the nineteenth century), the Everlasting Father" (of the "self-made" man), and (*teste* Mr. John Bright) the "Prince of Peace." The abstract symbol or expression for exchange-value, *money*, acquires a fictitious reality in proportion as exchange-value itself dominates the world; in other words, as commodities are produced for exchange and not for use, and on this basis, be it remembered, does our capitalistic system rest.

The third chapter of the present work contains an impassioned homily on "Prescription," which is said to be the sole safeguard against universal war, etc. The idea of "prescription" is apparently introduced to screen the present possessors of landed property which was originally confiscated from ecclesiastical and public lands. As an argument against "nationalisation" it is, however, singularly inept. It applies a principle which, in our anarchical society, rightly enough obtains as between one individual and another, to the relations of the individual to the community—a very different matter. The so-called "prescriptive right" simply means that mere possession gives a right to the individual possessing, as against any other individual, who cannot prove a greater right *quâ* individual. But as against society, prescription has no existence. "Society gave and society taketh away; blessed be the name of Society."

With respect to nationality, the principle of prescription is similar. So long as nationalism exists, each nation by virtue of established possession has the right to undisturbed enjoyment of its own territory as against any other nation. But once place politics on an international footing, and it is evident one nation will not be able to plead prescription against any measure decided upon (let us say) by the European or the world-federation for the common good. So much for M. Leroy-Beaulieu's attempted assimilation of the principle of individual to that of national land-ownership (see chap. v.)

We had noted many more things concerning M. Leroy-Beaulieu and his book for animadversion, but enough we think has been said to show its general character. Of course, we have the stock arguments, that the capitalist is an organiser of labour, that the difficulties of direction and organisation in a Socialist State would be insuperable, that Mr. Giffen, who is described as a "*statisticien très-exact*," says that the position of the working-classes is ameliorating, etc., etc. A great deal is made of the endeavour to prove that the "*grief historique*" of Marx is unfounded, because, forsooth, it is possible to discover other subsidiary causes contributing to the origination of the accumulation of capital besides those leading ones mentioned by Marx. We would observe in conclusion that the case of Scientific Socialism must be indeed strong, when a leading French economist like M. Leroy-Beaulieu, after having taken in hand the case against it, cuts so sorry a figure.

SOCIALISM AND RELIGION.

IT is sometimes said that Socialism is neither religious nor irreligious. This does not or should not mean that Socialism fails to come into contact with the views of the world and of life which the current religions furnish, or that at a particular stage in its progress it may not take up a position even of active hostility to those religions. What it means is that Socialism implies a state of society out and away beyond the barren speculative polemics of the hour.

The popular "Secularism" or "freethought" is simply the obverse side of the popular "dogmatic theology." In this it has the "reason of its being." With theology played out, Secularism is also played out. Like the two Kilkenny cats, Theology and Secularism must, in the long run, mutually devour each other.

Socialism is essentially neither religious nor irreligious, inasmuch as it re-affirms the unity of human life, abolishing the dualism which has lain at the foundation of all the great ethical religions. By this dualism I mean the antithesis of politics and religion, of the profane and the sacred, of matter and spirit, of this world and the "other world," and the various subordinate antagonisms to which these have given rise, or which they implicitly contain. Hitherto the whole tendency of our society and thought has been to make of aspects of things, distinguishable if you will, but not legitimately separable, separate and more or less opposed principles. We will take only the instance which most concerns the subject-matter of these remarks. Those feelings, aspirations, emotions (as we choose to call them) after the ideal which constitute the "religious sentiment" are very easily *distinguishable* from the impulses of kindliness, friendship, duty, etc., to individuals which ought to animate our daily life. They are distinguishable but not separable. Yet the current religions erect them into distinct principles. severing the "religious sentiment" from all connections with the world and human society, and transferring it to an imagined supernatural "world," which is nothing but a grotesque travesty of the relations of this world.

It is curious to trace how this came about. In the most ancient civilisations there is no separation between the political or social and the religious, simply because religion was then nothing more than the propitiation of dead ancestors, powers of nature, fetiches or other supposed supernatural agents (whose existence passed unquestioned to the human mind in its then stage) in the interests of the society. These ancestral ghosts, personified powers, or animated fetiches were as often immoral as not ; in fact, it would be more correct to say that for them morality and immorality had no existence. The worshipper possibly cared not one jot for them or they for him—his worship was a social duty. The only way in which they possessed any human interest was as embodying certain powers, which might be noxious or beneficent *to the State.* We have spoken of them as being "propitiated" and "worshipped," but it is doubtful if those terms can be applied with regard to the ancient religious cults more than very partially. The practices they embodied were rather those of compulsory invocation or regulation by means of magical spells and

4

incantations than prayers and " services " such as are
understood to-day. The social festivals were as much
religious as they were political. Political and religious
functions were necessarily united in the same persons
since every religious act was political, every political
act also religious.

The foregoing remarks apply in all essentials to
every primitive civilisation, to ancient India, Egypt,
China, Syria, Palestine. Even in later classical times,
religion was still a social and political matter, a thing
of this world only or mainly. The most sacred forms
of the Greek and Roman cults were those identified
with the preservation of the city, of the tribe, and of the
gens. Undoubting as was men's belief in the existence
of the supernatural, it only interested them in so far as
they conceived it to affect the community of which
they were a part. The supernatural, too, was as yet
imperfectly distinguished from the natural. There
was no religion of the supernatural *as such.* But with
the decay of the old civic morality and the absorption
of the small free States into centralised monarchies
and finally into the Roman Empire, men came to care
less and less for the body politic, and fell back more
and more upon themselves as individuals. At first
this individualism took the form of a search among the
leisured and educated class for the higher life of
wisdom. The Stoic, the Epicurean, and the Cynic had
each his special receipt for slipping through life as
comfortably as possible. But this, though satisfactory
for a time, palled in the long run. The Roman Empire
got ever more corrupt, its corruption ramifying through
all its branches; public life became more and more
vapid; the old religions, once instinct with meaning,
were but empty forms; the newer panaceas of the
philosophers failed to afford satisfaction. The utmost
they promised was to make the best of the doubtful
bargain—life.

But the sense of individualism was too strong for this merely negative creed. Men sought in vain for an object in life, collective or individual. In this state of mind they are confronted by a new Asiatic sect. They become initiated. At once the scene changes. This life is indeed pronounced hopelessly worthless. There is no citizenship here, no happiness for the individual, not even the apathy of the "wise man." But as this life crumbles into nothingness, there rises the fair vision of the "city of God," joys beyond imagination, not the "apathy" of "wisdom," but the "peace" of the blest. *Hic Rhodus, hic saltus!* Religion is henceforth separated from life, the religious sphere of *another* world is set over against the irreligious sphere of *this* world. Earth is drained of its ideal to feed Heaven. Society established on this basis involves the antagonisms of "temporal and spiritual" powers, of "world" and Church, of religious and profane, etc., etc. What is said applies not only to Christianity, but more or less to all the so-called ethical or universal religions, Zoroastrianism, Buddhism, Mahommedanism, etc. They are the expression of the decay of the old life, and hence they one and all centre in the individual and in another world, their concern with this world being purely incidental.

We daily see around us the result of 1,600 years of "other-worldliness" on character and conduct. Men and women upon whom the mere greed for gain palls are driven to the one ideal resource their education has given them or they can comprehend,—the hope of a glorified immortality for themselves. Those only who know from bitter experience the smile of honest contempt with which such people greet the idea of the sacrifice of personal or class privileges, or anything else for a social object, can appreciate the depth to which the canker has eaten into their souls. Yet it would be unjust to say that these people are bad.

They are religious and antisocial, just as there are
many others irreligious and antisocial.

In what sense Socialism is not religious will be
now clear. It utterly despises the "other world"
with all its stage properties—that is, the present
objects of religion. In what sense it is not irreligious
will be also, I think, tolerably clear. It brings back
religion from heaven to earth, which, as we have
sought to show, was its original sphere. It looks
beyond the present moment or the present individual
life though not, indeed, to another world, but to
another and a higher social life in this world. It is in
the hope and the struggle for this higher social life,
ever-widening, ever-intensifying, whose ultimate possi-
bilities are beyond the power of language to express or
thought to conceive, that the Socialist finds his ideal,
his religion. He sees in the reconstruction of society
in the interest of all, in the rehabilitation, in a higher
form and without its limitations, of the old communal
life—the proximate end of all present endeavour. We
take up the thread of Aryan tradition, but not where it
was dropped. The state or city of the ancient world
was one-sided, its freedom was political merely, based
on the slavery of the many; that of the future will be
democratic and social. It was exclusive, the union
within implied disunion without; the life of the
future will be international, cosmopolitan, in its scope.
Finally the devotion of its members was connected with
the existent supernatural belief, and involved a cultus;
the devotion of the member of the socialised community, like the devotion of all true Socialists to-day,
will be based on science and involve no cultus. In this
last point the religion of the Socialist differs from that
of the Positivist. The Positivist seeks to retain the
forms after the beliefs of which they are the expression
have lost all meaning for him. The Socialist whose
social creed is his only religion requires no travesty of

Christian rites to aid him in keeping his ideal before him.

In Socialism the current antagonisms are abolished, the separation between politics and religion has ceased to be, since their object-matter is the same. The highest feelings of devotion to the Ideal are not conceived as different in kind, much less as concerned with a different sphere, to the commoner human emotions, but merely as diverse aspects of the same fact. The stimulus of personal interest no longer able to poison at its source all beauty, all affection, all heroism, in short, all that is highest in us; the sphere of government merged in that of industrial direction; the limit of the purely industrial itself ever receding as the applied powers of Nature lessen the amount of human drudgery required; Art, and the pursuit of beauty and of truth ever covering the ground left free by the "necessary work of the world"—such is the goal lying immediately before us, such the unity of human interest and of human life which Socialism would evolve out of the clashing antagonisms, the anarchical individualism, religious and irreligious, exhibited in the rotting world of to-day—and what current religion can offer a higher ideal or a nobler incentive than this essentially human one?

SOCIALISM AND THE SUNDAY QUESTION.

THE question of a "free" Sunday is to no one more immediately important than to Socialists. For a proletariat strong in mind and in body is the first essential to the advent and the success of the revolution in this country as in every other. And no proletariat can be strong in mind or in body which is debarred from the opportunity of the full culture of either. The middle-class employer knows this right well when he protests against any infringement of the " day of rest." It was M. Guizot, so far as we remember, who in conversation with an English statesman sometime during the year 1848, remarked that the safety of England lay in her Sunday. Allowing for exaggeration, there is much truth in this assertion of the typical middle-class statesman of France. The " safety" of England from the point of view of its privileged classes has undoubtedly been conduced to by the British " Beer and Bible" Sunday. A well-conducted English workman, "thrifty and industrious," is no doubt kept in a state of dogged contentment by never knowing what leisure intelligently occupied means, by his tastes being carefully kept under, and by his weekly holiday being ' empty, swept, and garnished " of all relaxation. A man who knows nothing to interest him when he is free from work, naturally cares less about reduction of labour. It is culture in its widest sense which makes the revolutionist. By culture we do not mean the mere tools of education furnished by the School Board, but the habit of mind which forces a man beyond the *here* and the *now* of his own particular interests, or even of the events uppermost in the newspapers at the moment, and makes him feel a living interest and part in the past, the future, the distant. Now, it is the absence of *culture* in this sense which makes the English working classes safe and politically stable. While the French or German workman is occupied with "theories of the reorganisation of society," the English workman is content to keep his nose to the grindstone, heaping up, may be, a little competence for his old age (which will probably be consumed in the next industrial crisis, and certainly long before he *reaches* old age), and, when political, to concern himself with so-called "practical measures for the improvement of his class."

That the English Sunday is largely responsible for this state of affairs, we repeat, there is little doubt. But how came the Anglo-Saxon Sunday to be what it is? In mediæval times the Sunday was a day of recreation, of fairs, morris-dances, mystery plays, etc., and not of enforced idleness and gloom. The Puritan movement, which originated at the end of the sixteenth century in the reign of Elizabeth, gathering force and numbers till the rebellion which cost Charles I. his head embodied in its programme a strong antagonism to the old English Sunday,—an antagonism which was accentuated by the action of the opposite party who took an equally emphatic stand upon the Sunday of tradition. There was nothing merely arbitrary in the position adopted on either side. It was the extreme carrying out of what was involved in the respective attitudes of both parties. The Puritan movement was essentially a movement of the English middle-class, the yeomanry of the country, and the tradesmen of

the towns, against the remains of the mediaeval aristocratic and Church system. The attempt of Charles I.
to strengthen his prerogative—the ship-money, the
five members—only brought the crisis to an issue; its
causes lay far deeper. Protestantism, the new middle-
class version of Christianity, and Puritanism, the
insular commentary on this version, abolished the
festivals of Catholicism which had given the people
well-nigh as many additional holidays in the year as
there were Sundays. These old festival days were now
dedicated to work, and although all work was rigorously
interdicted on the Sabbath, so also was all pleasure.
This beautiful conception of a " day of rest " was
ratified by a Puritan Parliament in the well-known
Act of Charles II. Thenceforward the English Sunday
became the dreary day it is now.*

That it originated in the religious side of the English
middle-class revolution of the seventeenth century does
not mean that it has interfered with the material
interests of the middle-class. Their zeal for the
maintenance of the day as a " day of rest " does not
imply the disinterestedness which at first sight might
be supposed. More than a certain amount of work
in a year cannot be got out of the " human machine."
Thus, where, as on the Continent, there is no religious
or legal hindrance to Sunday labour, the weekly holiday
is obtained in the great industries just the same nevertheless, either on Sundays as in France, or where, as in
Austria, labour is the rule on that day, on Monday—
" blue Monday " as it is called. Now whether the leisure

---

* Puritanism, the insular guise of the larger movement of Protestantism which was the religious aspect of middle-class domination,
formally abolished the outward relation of religion to daily life.
Under Catholicism, the old-world feeling of the unity of human
interests still survived. Neither work nor amusement were altogether severed from religion. Puritanism finally separated them, and
the British Sunday, in which all work and amusement are alike pro-
hibited, is the expression of this separation.

(which the employer is forced to concede) be sacrificed
on the altar of middle-class creed, or be employed for
purposes of recreation or of instruction, does not
directly affect the pocket of the capitalist. But though
it does not directly affect him, it affects him very much
indirectly, as the English middle-classes have found
out. The man who through lack of something else to
do is induced to interest himself in the ministrations of
a Baptist chapel, is not so likely to be guilty of the
sin of discontent as the man who uses his leisure otherwise. And such a man is the ideal workman of the
British manufacturer.

To sum up the historical and actual aspects of the
question. In the Middle Ages, and indeed until production for profit became the motive power of the
world's life, religion secured at least a fourth of the
year in real holidays for the people ; while for the rest
the Church, which was the conservator of the amusements as it was of the learning of the time, often
interposed with effect to protect the serf from overwork.
This was the case in England, as elsewhere, before the
middle-class rising of 1642, subsequent to which the
religious aspect of the middle-class struggle in its
crudest form—viz., Puritanism, the cardinal doctrine of
which is the sinfulness of pleasure, suppressed the
catholic fête days of the old " merry England," as well
as the traditional amusements of Sunday. This
arrangement has proved so conducive to order and
good government that the institution of the British
" Sabbath " has rightly come to be regarded as one of
the bulwarks of capitalistic " order " in these islands.
The twaddle talked about the " Sabbath " protecting
the workman from exaction is seen in its true light
when we find that capitalism, in the long run, Sabbath
or no Sabbath, is compelled to concede one day's holiday
in the week ; and that the only difference is as to what
day it shall be and how that day shall be spent : points

which the dominant classes in this country arrogate to themselves the right of deciding.

In conclusion we would wish to point out what in our view is the true solution of the Sunday—or rather rest-day—question. And in this we claim to be speaking strictly within the range of "practical politics," and not from a more advanced standpoint ; for in a perfectly-organised socialist state where men never worked more than two or three hours a day, the whole question would lose much of its interest, and would practically solve itself. Now the fallacy which underlies the entire rationalistic defence for the English Sunday is the assumption that the whole world must rest on the *same* day if the whole world is to rest at all. This absurd notion of one *universal* holiday as the only alternative to none, is visible in the modern English equivalent for the mediæval festivals of St. Peter and St. Paul, to wit, that dedicated to the supreme deity or patron-saint of exchange, the Bank. Even here the tendency is for the whole machinery of labour to cease at once, while on Sunday this actually takes place as far as possible. Now, I ask, could anything be more irrational or more senseless than such a proceeding ? It is obvious if leisure is to be enjoyed usefully as regards mind or body some portion of the community must labour to enable the rest to profit by their holiday. Horrible injustice ! shriek the quondam humanitarian defenders of the British Sunday in chorus, you would make others work on the "day of rest" for your pleasure ! I answer we would give every single worker at least one day of rest a week; a blessing which a good many do not enjoy now (for all your English "Sabbath"), and cannot in the nature of things enjoy, do what you may, *while all are supposed to rest on the same day.* But we would surrender once and for all this chimerical notion of one day of universal rest, and institute three days a week, or, if necessary, more, as days of partial rest—*i.e.*, on which different sections of the community would be freed from labour in turn. In this way each section would be able really to profit, physically and mentally, by their leisure, inasmuch as they would have the advantage of the labour of the rest of the world, just as another day the rest of the world would have the advantage of their labour. Thus the " Sabbath " with its gloom would be for ever abolished and the weekly, bi-weekly, or tri-weekly holiday could be made a day of real enjoyment for all.

THE MODERN REVOLUTION.

A LECTURE TO A MIDDLE-CLASS AUDIENCE.

THERE is an old German legend, embodied in a well-known poem, which relates how, in the days when Prussia and Austria were rent by the feuds of king and empress, there lived in a quiet country town of the former country the maiden Leonora, whose lover, Wilhelm, was away, fighting with Frederick's army. One day, the legend relates, when for a long time no tidings had been heard of him, news came of the battle of Prague, and of the conclusion of peace, and following thereupon arrived the victorious troops on their way home. But among all the host Wilhelm is looked for in vain; there is none who can tell what fate has befallen him. Leonora knows no consolation. In a moment of despairing grief she throws herself on the ground and blasphemes heaven. At nightfall a charger in full speed is heard, and at the gate a rider dismounts. He calls to Leonora to dress quickly, for

> " Thou must ride a hundred leagues this night,
>   My nuptial couch to share."

She mounts the charger in haste. In furious gallop they hurry along, amid a cloud of dust and showers of sparks. As they whirl o'er heath and bog and road, the ravens flap their wings, the bells toll, the frogs croak in chorus. There passes a funeral procession,

and a spectral rabble dancing round a gibbet sweep
along in their train. At cock-crow they reach a graveyard, when, in an instant, the rider's mantle and jerkin
fall in pieces, disclosing no Wilhelm, but a skeleton
with scythe and hour-glass. The charger vanishes in
flame. Wails issue from an open grave, into which
Leonora sinks, while, in the moonlight, phantoms
dance around in giddy circles; the burden of their
song :—

> "Thy body's knell we toll;
> May God preserve thy soul!"

We may, I think, in the story of Leonora's ride
possibly find some parallel to the history of humanity
in this nineteenth century. The civilisation in whose
embrace we have been clasped, and whose mantel has
been covering us, and of whose praises we are never
tired : what is its nature? What is beneath that fair-
seeming jerkin; is it a thing of flesh and blood or is it
a ghastly skeleton? Whither is it leading us—to an
idyllic love-scene or to a graveyard and a tomb? Will
the steed on which we are dashing forward, as we
fondly imagine, to untold havens of commercial bliss,
vanish in flame—it may chance of nitro-glycerine or of
some other flame—or will it endure?

These are the questions involved in our subject of
to-night, and they are questions which, in some form or
other, are being asked by all thinking men in the
present day. The majority will concede that we are
passing through a period of change, though the true
meaning of that change they may not be so willing to
admit.

It is our business now to examine briefly the nature
of the stuff or raw material that is woven into our state
system, our manners and customs, and even our
religion. A moment's glance at these elements of
our civilisation will show us that they have as their
material basis two institutions, viz.: land-ownership

and capital. With the principle of land-ownership
I do not propose especially to detain your attention
to-night; firstly, because it has been dealt with at
length—though it is true nowhere thoroughly—in
many recent works which, doubtless, many present have
read; and, secondly, because the existence of private
property in land, important as it is, is really of minor
importance to the existence of a capitalistic mode
of production. Hence into the fallacy of the theory of
which we have heard so much lately, that the mere
confiscation of competition rents would effect any vast
change in our civilisation, I do not propose to enter
otherwise than by implication.

The foregoing, then, are the factors constituting the
texture of our social system—the mantle in which we
are enwrapped. Steam, electricity—the inventions,
the discoveries, the vast development of machinery
distinguishing the nineteenth century from all other
ages—these things are the steed bearing us along the
giddy whirl of modern life. The middle-class man,
the merchant, the manufacturer or his hanger-on,
dreams of the universal spread of this, his civilisation;
with its churches and chapels; its missionary organisations "for spreading the light of the gospel into
foreign parts;" its shunting-yards; its factory-
chimneys; its trans-continental railways; its West-
end houses; its suburban villas; as the end of all
progress, the bourne of humanity. In his impetuous
course he never thinks of stopping to ask the question,
"What is happiness? What is the ideal having
possession of me? What is the hope I am clasping?"
Like Leonora, human nature has been deprived of its
ideal; the dream of classicism, of the ideal city, or of
the perfect life of wisdom, has passed away. The dream
of the mediæval monk, of the perfect life after death
in communion with a supra-mundane godhead and a
company of glorified saints, has passed away also, so

far as constituting a practical life-object for men is concerned. Commercialism in the shape of money, capital, competition, success in life, has, in the mock vesture of an ideal, summoned the human Leonora to a reckless ride to an unknown bourne. The summons has been accepted with unquestioning faith—a faith so unquestioning that the cry of the frogs and the ravens; the gibbet, crime; the ever-increasing phantom crew —starvation, misery, disease, and pauperism—go for nothing as they scour along in mad career in the track, mocking the rider. It remains to tear asunder the vesture of our hypothetical Wilhelm and to discover whether he be real or spectral. We shall, I think, in this disclose another line of parallel to the legend; we shall find, namely, that he is indeed a hideous skeleton, heartless, eyeless, the issue of a blasphemy, not against any god, perhaps, but against what are higher than any god—the principles of justice and truth.

In doing this I shall have first of all to call your attention to the following dry statement of figures. The annual production of the United Kingdom amounts roughly to thirteen hundred millions. Of this, ten hundred millions are absorbed by the minority (as regards population) of capitalists, landowners, and the middle classes generally, leaving three hundred millions only for the working classes, *i.e.*, at once for the bulk of the community and those classes that make the wealth. The land-owners of the country take out of the thirteen hundred millions, directly, only one hundred and thirty-five millions, while at least half of this income is mortgaged back to the capitalist class for loans. So that the amount absorbed by land-ownership, as such, is by no means so important an item as some would have us believe.

Such, then, are the facts. The major part of the wealth of the community is absorbed in the form of interest or profit; or, in other words, in the circulation of money as capital. It remains to investigate the true meaning of this circulation of money as capital. It is, I imagine, unnecessary to enter at length into the well-known economic distinction of utility-value— the value which the commodity possesses in its consumption,—and exchange-value, the value which it possesses in the market; it will suffice to say that— commodities simply representing the result of labour —value in a strictly economical sense means nothing more than the differential amount of labour that they severally embody. Hence value *per se* has but one quality, that of being the embodiment of labour; its differences being in point of quantity alone. For this reason the value of one commodity can be expressed in the substance of another; the value of a particular quantity of linen can be expressed in a coat, for example.

The ultimate issue of the various forms in which value may be represented is the money form. In this form the value of any commodity from out the complex of commodities is embodied, not in any other commodity from out this complex, but in a *tertium quid*. This *tertium quid* is money. Thus, a pound sterling is the sign and symbol of a definite amount of concrete labour—it matters not in what commodity it may be embodied—whether in a coat, in ten ells of linen, in five pounds of tea, in ten pounds of coffee, in a quarter of wheat, or in a quarter of a ton of iron. The sole primary function of money is, to act as a medium of exchange, on the primitive system of barter becoming impracticable or inconvenient. Instead, therefore, of the simple and direct barter of one commodity for another, we have now a third term interposed, *the process of exchange becomes indirect*. One commodity is sold, *i.e.*, is parted with for money, and the other commodity purchased with that money. But the appearance upon the scene of a standard of value,

a commodity having no other than an exchange value, *i.e.*, possessing no utility value in itself, carries with it remarkable and unforeseen consequences. " With the possibility of obtaining commodities in the form of pure exchange value, or *vice versâ*," says Karl Marx, the founder of the new Socialist economy, " The greed for gold awakens. With the extension of the circulation of commodities, the power of gold grows; the ever-ready, unconditionally social form of riches. Through gold, said Christopher Columbus, one could even get souls into paradise." Circulation—in other words, the indirect process of exchange—is the great social retort into which everything flows, to come out crystallised into money in some form or shape. The issue of this is, that the original money-formula, which we may represent thus :—first term, Commodity ; second term, Money ; third term, Commodity again—becomes supplemented by another and far more recondite process. This second process is that of buying in order to sell again, changing money for money ; and may be expressed by another formula, of which the first term is Money ; the second Commodity ; and the third Money again. The entry of this second money-process upon the arena denotes the transition of money, or exchange-value pure and simple, into capital. For, since money has no utility-value but only an exchange-value, which is, of course, uniform as to quality, there can be nothing gained by the process except it be in point of quantity. And in fact, money circulating in this way does gain in quantity. In short, the movement or circulation of money as capital has for its end the return of the money, *plus an increment.**
This increment is termed by Karl Marx *surplus value.*

* This, of course, does not mean that in every individual case an increment is realised. There may be a loss in any particular instance. But the loss of any particular capitalist is a corresponding gain to other capitalists. It is not a loss to capital, or to the capitalist class. Labour, or the labouring class, does not benefit by it.

5

But now arises the question, 'By what process of economical magic is this result obtained? Where does the increment or surplus value, which is the source of profit, come from?' It cannot come out of exchange-value or money itself. Every capitalist cannot have the advantage of every other capitalist. The mere circulation cannot effect this marvellous change. It must therefore be looked for outside the circulating medium, or the capital. But the complimentary factor to capital in all production is labour. Hence it is from labour— or, to put it concretely, from the labourer—that the surplus value must be derived; but, to this end, the labourer's capacity for labour, his *labour-force*, must come into the market as any other commodity. Now, the value of labour-force or working power is determined, like that of every other commodity, by the average time necessary to its production or reproduction. Again: this labour-force exists only as a quality of a living individual; but to the existence and maintenance of a living individual a certain supply of the means of living is necessary. Hence, the value of labour-force resolves itself into the value of a determinate supply of the means of living, and changes with the value of these means of living, *i.e.*, with the length of time necessary for their production. This fact furnishes the magic thread to the unravelment of the woof of the whole modern capitalistic system:

"That half-a-day's work," says Marx, "is necessary to "maintain the workman in life during the twenty-"four hours, does not in any way prevent him from "working a whole day. The value of labour-force, "and its exploitation in the process of labour, are two "distinct quantities. The first determines its exchange "value, the second its utility-value. This difference "the capitalist has in his eye in purchasing labour-"force. Its useful characteristic, that of making thread "or boots, was merely a *sine quâ non*, because labour

" must be expended in a useful form to make value.
" The decisive element was the specific utility-value of
" the commodity, labour, that of being the source of
" value and of more value than it has itself. This is
" the specific service the capitalist requires of it. And
" he acts thereby in accordance with the eternal laws
" regulating the exchange of commodities. . . . The
" capitalist has foreseen this situation ' das ihn lachen
" macht.' Hence the workman finds in the workroom
" the necessary means of production, not for a six, but
" a twelve hours' process of labour.

" The second period of the process of work, beyond
" the boundaries of this necessary work, though it costs
" him work, expenditure of labour-force, yet realises
" no value for him. It realises a surplus value, that
" smiles on the capitalist with all the charm of a
" creation out of nothing. I call this portion of the
" working day *surplus working time*, and the work
" expended thereon *surplus labour*. It is as important
" for the knowledge of surplus value to understand
" it as a mere flux of surplus working time, as merely
" embodied surplus work, as it is for a knowledge of value
" generally to understand it as mere flux of working
" time, as mere embodied work. Only the form, in which
" this surplus work is extracted from the immediate
" producer, the labourer, distinguishes the various econo-
" mical formations of society, for instance, a society
" founded on slavery from one based on wage labour.

" John Stuart Mill observes, in his ' Principles of
" Political Economy,' that it is questionable if all the
" mechanical inventions yet made have lightened the
" day's toil of any human being. Such is, however,
" by no means the object of machinery as applied under
" the capitalist system. Like every other development
" of the productive power of labour, its object is to
" cheapen commodities, and to shorten that portion of
" the working day which the workman has for himself,

" in order to lengthen the other part of the working
" day which he gives to the capitalist for nothing.   It
" is a means to the production of surplus value.

" The capitalist has purchased labour-force at its
" current rate.   Hence its utility-value belongs to him
" during a working day.   He has acquired the right to
" make the workman labour for him during the day.
" But what is the working day?   At all events less
" than the actual day.   By how much?   The capitalist
" has his eye on this *ultima thule*, the necessary limits
" of the working day.   As capitalist he is only
" personified capital.   His soul is the soul of capital.
" But capital has but a single impulse in life, that of
" realising itself as surplus-value, creating surplus
" value, and with its constant factor the means of pro-
" duction, of sucking in the greatest possible amount
" of surplus value.   Capital is dead labour, which
" lives vampire-like by sucking in living labour, and
" lives the better, the more it sucks in.   The time
" during which the workman labours is the time during
" which the capitalist consumes the labour-force pur-
" chased from him.   If the workman consumes his
" available time for himself, he robs the capitalist.
" The capitalist falls back upon the law regulating the
" exchange of commodities.   He, like every other
" purchaser, seeks to wring the greatest possible use
" out of the utility-value of his commodity.

" But suddenly the voice of the workman, drowned
" in the storm and stress of the process of production,
" makes itself heard :—The commodity which I have
" sold to you is distinguished from all other com-
" modities by its creating a utility-value greater than
" it costs itself.   This was the reason why you bought
" it.   What appears on your side as realisation of
" capital, appears on my side as superfluous expenditure
" of my labour-force.   You and I recognise on the
" arena of the market but one law, that of the exchange

"of commodities (supply and demand). And the
" consumption of the commodity does not belong to
" the seller, who delivers it, but to the buyer who
" acquires it. To you belongs, therefore, the use of
" my daily labour-force. But by means of its daily
" sale-price I must daily reproduce it, and hence can
" sell it anew. Apart from natural decay through old
" age, etc., I must be able to work again to-morrow in
" the same normal condition of power, health and
" freshness as to-day. You are continually preaching
" to me the gospel of ' saving ' and 'abstinence.' Good!
" I will, like a sensible, saving, business man, preserve
" my only faculty, my labour-force, and abstain from
" any foolish expenditure of it. I will only spend as
" much of it—daily convert as much of it into work—
" as is consistent with its normal continuance and
" healthy development. By a measureless lengthening
" of the working day, you use up more of my labour-
" force than I can replace in three days. What you
" thus gain in work I lose in the substance of work.
" Using my labour-force and robbing me of it are
" quite different things. I demand, therefore, a working
" day of normal length, and I demand it without any
" appeal to your heart, for in money matters compassion
" has no place. You may be a model citizen, perhaps
" a member of the Society for the Prevention of Cruelty
" to Animals, and stand in the odour of sanctity in
" addition, but the thing that you represent to me
" carries no heart in its breast. What seems to beat
" therein is my own hearts pulse. I demand a normal
" working day, because I demand the value of my
" commodity like every other vendor."

Hence the modern economic *régime* must be a perpetual strife. The capitalist maintains his rights as a
buyer to make the working day as long as possible, and
the workman maintains his right as seller to limit the
working day.

And now, before concluding this portion of our subject, I have a word to say on the argument employed
to account for the existence and action of capital by
the current economist.* Interest, it is said, is the
reward of abstinence. Now the conception of capital,
as we have seen, has its root in the conception of
money. Money—which is nothing more than the
abstract expression for all possible commodities, *i.e.*,
products of labour — has become hypostasised, and
acquired a special, material value and function of its
own, apart from its merely formal value as a medium of
exchange. This hypostasis found its crudest theoreti-
cal expression in the infancy of economic science as
the mercantile theory (so-called); but the same fallacy,
in a practical and far more insidious form, underlies the
orthodox economic idea of capital, which, as we have
shown, consists in the ascription to money of a faculty
of quantitative increase in the mere course of circulation, a faculty which it does not and cannot in itself
possess.

Economists, in the vain search for a scientific explanation of interest on capital, lighted upon the naïvely
brilliant idea that *interest* was the reward a beneficent
Nature had provided for "*thrift.*" Now, as every
small boy knows, if he abstains from eating his
cake, or a portion of it, one day, he has the pleasure of
consuming the same another day. But the only reward
of the small boy's virtuous thrift is the future pleasure of
consumption as against the present or past. With
this he has to be satisfied, as the cake does not increase
or multiply with keeping. But we are asked by the
economists to believe that the virtue of the small
boy, like Samson's locks, grows with his growth and
strengthens with his strength, insuchwise that when
he becomes a big capitalist it has acquired proportions
entitling it to a reward altogether incommensurate
with what satisfied it in its earlier stages. Now he

---

* Profit is divided by economists into three elements : (1) wages of
superintendence, (2) indemnification for risk, (3) reward for abstinence.

expects his cake, under the abstract expression, "commodity in general," or its concrete symbol money, to grow by keeping to indefinable proportions, like the good fairy's cake in the nursery tale. So far, so good; but here the uninitiated stumbles across the puzzling fact that to the carnal eye the abstinence and the increment do not run hand in hand together, but that the abstinence lags behind the increment, and finally stops altogether, and that, too, just at the time when the pace of the increment is accelerating by "leaps and bounds." To the carnal eye, for example, the abstinence of a Nathaniel Rothschild or a Samuel Morley is below the *minimum visibile*. The unfortunate student of orthodox economy is thus driven to accept the economist's assurance on the strength of that unsatisfactory surrogate the "eye of faith." Given a causal relation between abstinence and increment, he naturally expects to find, *cæteris paribus*, a progressive increase in the cause to precede or accompany a progressive increase in the effect. Experience, however, shows the reverse. What, then, becomes of abstinence as a scientific *raison d'être* of interest? * Surely, it is something like effrontery for a doctrine which has at its basis such childishness as this, to arrogate to itself the name of science, as is done by the orthodox economy.

We have, I think, seen the mantle and jerkin of our Wilhelm fall piece by piece. We have disclosed no warm-blooded hero showing the earnest of a nobler life of progress in the higher human attributes, but the grinning skull of fraud and force.

Let us now look back for a few moments upon history, and see whether what we have arrived at logically is borne out politically and historically. As all of you are doubtless aware, the industrial system of antiquity was founded on slavery; production was carried on entirely, or almost entirely, by slaves. This system of slave industry became gradually modified,

* The same applies to "wages" of superintendence and "indemnification for risk." The "wages" become greatest when the capitalist ceases to "superintend;" and the "indemnification" reaches its highest point when the possessor of wealth can afford to defy all risk with impunity.

after the disruption of the Roman Empire, into serfage.
Slaves could not now be bought or sold at pleasure, but
were inseparable, in most cases, from the land on which
they were born.   Hence it was the interest of the
feudal lord of the soil to maintain them as far as
possible in a healthy and contented condition, since, if
by ill-treatment he diminished their numbers or im-
paired their labour-power, he was himself the loser by
it.   With the decline of the mediæval system and the
rise of towns a new industrial organisation appeared—
that of guilds of independent burghers.   The township
got the feudal services of the citizens within its
boundaries commuted for an annual tribute.   In this
way free labour arose; each man now worked for himself and his family at a particular handicraft to which
the guild supplied a regular training.   In this way too
an organised system of distribution—of commerce—
came into existence; although, and this cannot be too
strongly insisted upon, the interest of production
still primarily centred in the utility and the goodness
of the product itself, rather than in the profit realis-
able on it in exchange.   Leagues for mutual protection
against the military robbers of the period were formed,
of which the most important was the famous Hanseatic
League.   With the Renaissance, and still more the
Reformation, the main strength of the mediæval
system pure and simple was broken up.   The middle
classes of the towns became more and more powerful,
and, with their power, more and more restive at the
imposts laid upon them, and at the restriction of their
liberty and dignity by governments constituted of the
aristocratic lords of the soil, and of the crown with
its advisers.*   Risings took place in various parts of
Europe; as, for instance, the Fronde in France, the

---

* The individual burgher, it must be remembered, had no significance in the mediæval hierarchy.   The township as a whole was alone
recognised as entering into the larger system of the mediæval world.

civil war between King and Parliament in England; the earliest of these anti-feudal risings was the revolt in the Netherlands under the Artevelds, in the fourteenth century.

The growing breach between the "Commons," or "Third Estate,"—a name originally applied to the smaller land-holders,—as the trading classes now came to be called, and the two feudal estates, consisting respectively of the superior clergy (bishops and archbishops, etc.), and the nobility, surmounted by the crown with its councillors, culminated in the great French Revolution of 1789. In this revolution the third estate was arrayed against the clergy, the nobility, and the sovereign. The monarchy, which in the feudal system was merely the crowning of the edifice, had, on the first symptoms of decay in that system, endeavoured to utilise the anomalous state of things thence arising for the strengthening of its prerogative. This was attempted with varying success by well-nigh all the sovereigns of England from Henry VIII. to Charles I., and was successfully accomplished by Louis XIV. of France; but on the outbreak of the great French Revolution all jealousy between monarchy and aristocracy was banished throughout Europe in the face of the threatening danger from the third estate; but burgher and noble—or, as the French have it, *bourgeois* and *grand seigneur*—in their struggles for supremacy were oblivious of the rise above the social horizon of "a cloud no bigger than a man's hand," in the shape of a new political factor—a fourth estate—destined to prove a menace alike to both their interests. This fourth estate, distinct from the peasantry of the country, as the new commonalty or third estate, was distinct from the land-holding commonalty or yeomanry of feudal times, was none other than the modern Proletariat or working-class.

On the first rise of the town system every tradesman

(burgher or citizen) combined in his own person or immediate household the functions of workman, supervisor, and distributor, wholesale and retail; but with the development of industry these functions became separated, and with their separation the distinction between employer and employé, master and workman, *bourgeois* and *prolétaire*, arose. This distinction, although apparent socially from the sixteenth century, first became definitely marked in a political sense during the course of the French Revolution. In its earlier stages the Girondist party may be roughly characterised as that of the middle classes against the "Mountain," or Jacobin party, round which the working classes rallied: but on the fall of the Girondist faction, and the supremacy of the popular party, it was discoverable that the so-called party of the Mountain itself consisted for the most part of men such as Robespierre, St. Just, and their followers, *i.e.*, men who represented only a further phase of the revolution of the third estate, or middle class. One leader only can be named at this time who clearly grasped the situation, and deservedly won the confidence of the people, alike for his political insight and his honesty of purpose, and this man was Jean Paul Marat. After the reaction had set in throughout Europe, *i.e.*, at the beginning of the present century, party lines became definitely set on the new class basis. The capitalistic or middle classes were unconsciously driven to feel the necessity of a compromise with the landed aristocracy. This compromise took the form of constitutional government, in which Teryism, or landed interest, and Liberalism, or capitalistic interest, took it by turns to prey upon the people. The prodigious development of capitalism in this century—the polarisation of wealth and luxury on the one hand (oftentimes colossal fortunes realised in a few years) and starvation on the other—in short, the exhibition of the class

antagonism between capitalist and workman reaching
proportions dwarfing all other class-distinctions, is due
to the transformation of the whole process of industrial
production by what, up to the present time, has proved
the greatest curse mankind has ever suffered under,
viz., machinery. To machinery we owe the factory
system with all its attendant horrors. This replace-
ment of the old *petite industrie* by the new *grande
industrie*, it is needless to say, is the greatest economic
revolution the world has yet seen, and to this, modern
Capitalism and modern Socialism alike owe their origin.
When production was on a small scale the individual
owning his own tools, etc., and producing primarily for
the use of himself and family, and only secondarily for
exchange, the latter, simple and direct as it was, lay in
his own control. Under the capitalistic system this is
no longer so. The producer is now entirely dependent
for his capacity to produce on conditions altogether
outside himself and his immediate surroundings.

In the factory, the mill, the workshop, the mine, the
farm, etc., each producer is, so to speak, a cog in one of
the wheels of a complex system. The stoppage of the
smallest of these wheels affects the whole mechanism of
the particular branch of industry to which it belongs,
and in some cases of all other branches. Economic production has become a social function. It has passed
completely out of the hands of the individual as an
individual. At the same time, while the exchange of
the product has also passed out of the control of the
individual producer himself, it has not passed into that
of the collective body of producers as in the nature of
things it ought, but rather into the hands of other
individuals, who are for the most part in no way concerned with the process of production as such, but who
possess and control the land, machinery, etc., *i.e.*, the
conditions of production. The same with distribution.
The function of distribution, wholesale and retail, has

not only become definitely separated from that of production, but the gain of the distribution accrues not to
the immediate distributor, but to him who controls the
material conditions of distribution, in other words, to
the capitalist.   As a result of the incompatibility of a
collective production with an exchange for the benefit
of individuals, and regulated by individual greed, we
have an ever-increasing wealth for the few, an ever-
increasing poverty for the many.

As a consequence of the economic change described,
the old war between the third estate, the *bourgeois*, or
middle class on the one side, and the aristocracy and
clergy on the other, which was the main issue in the
French Revolution, has been replaced to-day by another
class war, that of *bourgeois* and *proletaire*, or employer
and workman.   This is a war between the producers and
the trading, or capitalist class, whose " hangers-on " the
landowners have become.

We have spoken of the way in which Capitalism with
its immediate result, competition, indirectly ramifies
throughout our whole social system, affecting not only
its direct victims, the workers, but the middle classes
themselves.   Its physiological effect is seen in the
prevalence of mental and nervous disease, in short-
ness of life and in a generally lower physical tone than
that characterising former ages.   Its moral effect is seen
in (1) the prevalent spirit of universal distrust and
suspicion necessarily generated by the desire of every
man to outbid his neighbour ; and still worse (2) in the
organised hypocrisy which pervades our social life.
The good man, the clear-sighted man, dare not express
his views, much less act up to them, lest, forsooth, he
should be ruined by the withdrawal of the patronage of
the knaves or fools upon whom he is dependent for his
livelihood.   There are, doubtless, some present who can
personally corroborate my statement in this matter.

The political pendant of Capitalism is annexation,

with its slaughter of helpless savages; its poisoning of them by bad spirits; its openings up of commercial centres; in short, its extension of empire at all cost in its mad hunt for markets in which to disgorge its surplus produce, and posts in which to "place" the younger sons of its governing classes. Just as the inevitable tendency of Capitalism industrially is for independent smaller capitalists to be absorbed into a few large firms, so it is its tendency politically for small free states to be sucked into great empires.

Finally, the religious aspect of our capitalistic civilisation is dogmatic Protestantism. The Reformation which began among the middle classes has continued, generally speaking, to coincide with them. The predominantly commercial states of Christendom are the predominantly Protestant ones, while even in Catholic countries the main strength of the Protestant minority lies in the trading classes. The religious creed of the capitalist *bourgeoisie* is dogma, *minus* sacerdotalism. The religious creed of the land-owning aristocracy is sacerdotalism, with a nominal adhesion to dogma. The watchword of one is, an infallible Church; the standard of the other, an infallible Bible. The Romish or High-Anglican squire represents incarnate land, on its religious side; the Baptist haberdasher, incarnate capital.

But it is unnecessary to particularise. What is our whole system? What is Constitutionalism but (as we before said) a compact between Land and Capital, whereby the one agrees to subserve the interests of the other? The Conservative land-owner pledges himself to support the Liberal capitalist in his self-interested reforms, and the Liberal capitalist promises to preserve intact for the Conservative land-owner the fundamental bases of hereditary privilege. And so the game has gone merrily on, barring little quarrels now and then, for a century past.

And now we come to the question, What is to be the

end of these things? The polarisation of wealth and
poverty goes on daily. We hasten towards a cata-
strophe of some kind. The weight of capital must
sooner or later become intolerable, for the simple
reason that the tendency is for its worst features to
become more and more marked, while with the natural
increase of the population, the workers become less and
less able to cope with them. What Karl Marx calls the
"reserve army of industry," that floating mass of population just on the verge of starvation and ready to work
for wages which mean death within a few years, is daily
and hourly augmenting. To the question so commonly
asked us, "What do you propose as a succedaneum to
the present system?" our answer is, the only lasting
alternative, and, indeed, the necessary issue, logical and
historical, of the present situation—that, therefore, for
which the working classes have to strive, is nothing less
than for Communism or a collectivist Socialism; understanding by this the assumption by the people, in other
words, the concentration in the hands of a democratic
state, of land, raw material, instruments of production,
funded capital, etc., insuchwise that each citizen shall
obtain the full advantage of the improved processes of
production, inasmuch as each citizen shall have to con-
tribute his share to the necessary work of society.

A calculation has been made by Mr. William Hoyle
(a non-Socialist) that were every person to do this,
under a scientifically organised system, and with the
highly-developed machine-power we possess properly
applied, the working day might be reduced to somewhat less than two hours—i.e., that this time would
suffice to supply us with all the necessities and real
comforts of life, only excluding useless luxury. It
must be remembered that under a properly organised
industrial system the number of those claiming wages
of superintendence would be incalculably reduced, thus
freeing for productive purposes large numbers of hands

now practically, although not nominally, idle. The
same may be said with even greater force of distribution. The waste of labour in these two departments,
in the present disorganised state of industry, is so
enormous as to strike every thinking man. The work
involved in them would, moreover, be remunerated on
the same basis as that of production pure and simple,
and not at fancy-tariffs as at present.

This applies also to what is known as the labour of
scarcity-talent. It may seem to those accustomed to
the present system an injustice that the clever doctor,
advocate, artist, author or composer should be able to
absorb no more of the good things of life than the man
of average ability. This is only one of the countless
instances of custom perverting the mental, or rather
moral, vision. The theorem that it is just for Society
(the moral order) to stereotype and intensify the
inequalities of Nature (the pre-moral order) is only
defensible on a new rendering of the " to-him-that-
hath-shall-be-given-and-he-shall-have-more-abun-
dantly" principle. Why the man who possesses
faculties which must of themselves bring him " honour,
love, obedience, troops of friends," besides the joys of
original creation and the intrinsic sense of power that
the mere possession of such faculties involves, should
expect, in addition to all these things and by way of
right, to have a lion's share of mere material luxuries,
is perhaps one of the strangest moral phenomena
engendered by our intrinsically immoral social state.
The natural and unperverted moral sense would seem
to declare for the very reverse, namely, that inasmuch
as the gifted man is placed by nature on a higher level
than the ordinary man, a circumstance which must, to
some extent at least, render him independent of the
things which concern the peace of the latter, he should
the rather forego a portion of his own legitimate share
in such things. The utmost, however, that is contem-

plated by the Socialist is his being placed on an *equal* economical footing with his naturally inferior brother.

The aim of Socialism is thus to organise a collective existence for Humanity—to replace the lower, the *physically disordered* "*struggle for existence*" by the higher, the *intelligently ordered* "*co-operation for existence.*" Socialism would at a blow root out the cancer *competition*, which is consuming the vitals of society, " the iron law " by which wages are reduced to starvation point, and thus the greater part of civilised mankind are condemned to perpetual slavery, and the remainder degraded in other ways physically, intellectually, and morally. The craving for wealth,—fortune-making as an end in life—would die of inanition since it would be impossible for any human being to make a fortune. Men would be driven to the cultivation of higher intellectual aims once the lower were effectually removed from their grasp. For by Socialism the real source of physical and moral degradation, which is not the craving for drink we hear so much of, but the even more repulsive craving for gain and material success, a craving which permeates the whole of society, not excepting the (so-called) higher professions, would be dried up.

The collective existence we speak of must inevitably, in the end, become international. Not only the mere geographical boundaries of statesmen will lose meaning, but even the national distinctions of race and language will become absorbed in the larger unity of the socialised world. For with a socialist *régime* established throughout the world the *raison d'être* of nationalism and of statesmanship would be at an end. Be-decorated cowards whose claims to recognition rest upon their ability to sit in a comfortable saloon or tent well out of harm's reach and order the bombardment of a practically defenceless town or the slaughter of ill-armed barbarians, so far from being allowed to steal public money through the agency of their friends, the governing classes, in the shape of pensions, would sink to their just level of contempt among men. The workers of all nations (*i.e.*, the thinking portion of them), who now feel that their interests are one, would then practically give effect to that doctrine of " human solidarity" till now but a mere phrase. Our whole modern system of production, exchange, communication, education, which though essentially *international*, is used for *national* ends (just as our essentially *socialised* system of industry is used for *individual* ends) would then be completely internationalised.

Socialism has been well described as a new conception of the world presenting itself in industry as co-operative Communism, in politics as international Republicanism, in religion as atheistic Humanism, by which is meant the recognition of social progress as our being's highest end and aim. The establishment of society on a Socialistic basis would imply the definitive abandonment of all theological cults, since the notion of a transcendent god or semi-divine prophet is but the counterpart and analogue of the transcendent governing-class. So soon as we are rid of the desire of one section of society to enslave another, the dogmas of an effete creed will lose their interest. As the religion of slave industry was Paganism ; as the religion of serfage was Catholic Christianity, or Sacerdotalism ; as the religion of Capitalism is Protestant Christianity or Biblical Dogma ; so the religion of collective and co-operative industry is Humanism, which is only another name for Socialism.

There is a party who think to overthrow the current theology by disputation and ridicule. They fail to see that the theology they detest is so closely entwined with the current mode of production that the two things must stand or fall together—that not until the establishment of a collectivist *régime* can the words of Algernon Charles Swinburne be fulfilled :—

6

> " Though before thee the throned Cytherean
>   Be fallen and hidden her head,
> Yet thy kingdom shall pass, Galilean,
>   Thy dead shall go down to the dead."

But ere we reach our reconstruction we have the last
agonised throes of Revolution to pass through. The
privileged classes, it is too much to hope, will surrender
without a struggle. But we are nearing the catas-
trophe. Our churches and chapels, our prisons, our
reformatories, our workhouses, may be full to over-
flowing, but the end is approaching. Already the
discerning may see the open tomb in the distance,
already hear the chant of the goblins of destiny indicating the termination of the mad chase and the
dissolution, it may be by a quiet euthanasia, it may be
in blood and fire, of the ghastly mockery of human
aspiration we call "the civilisation of the nineteenth
century.'

CONSCIENCE AND COMMERCE.

WE often come across a species of virtuous indignation which is apt to be aroused by some tale of the woes of a railway company whom the wicked passenger "defrauds" by travelling without having previously paid his fare. "Strange," it is said (and we find the sentiment commonly repeated whenever the subject comes up in the Press), "that a man who would scorn to rob his neighbour in his individual capacity, yet will not hesitate to 'defraud' a company;" for it is acknowledged to be by such persons that the bulk of these "frauds" (so-called) are perpetrated. The inconsistency of such a proceeding is then enlarged upon with all due emphasis.

This, in itself, comparatively unimportant incident of modern life, opens up a curious ethico-economical problem. Two things are quite clear. One is that a considerable section of persons instinctively feel a difference between their moral relations to individual men and women and their relations to a joint-stock company. The other is that the ordinary middle-class intellect cannot see any reason for this distinction, and having possibly a sense of the instability to commercial relations which would ensue from its recognition, adopts the high moral tone. Yet it is doubtful if even the most hardened *bourgeois* does not really feel that there *is* a difference between stealing a neighbour's coat and "defrauding" a joint-stock company, unwilling as he may be to acknowledge it.

Now the question is on what is this feeling of distinction based. It must have some explanation. We may as well state at once our conviction that it is based on the fact that in the one case there is a *real* moral relation involved, while in the other there is only a *fictitious* one—a fact which inherited moral instinct recognises, but, the reason sophisticated by the economic forms of modern society and the artificial morality necessary to them, refuses to admit.

We do not intend entering upon any elaborate discussion on the basis of ethics. But we suppose that every one will concede that the essence of moral relation is that it is between concretes—between one concrete individual and another, or else between that individual and the concrete social organism of which he forms a part. It is plain we cannot owe a duty either to an inanimate object or to an abstraction, as such. We speak, it is true, of "duty to the cause," but this is only a metaphor; we really mean duty to the oppressed humanity of to-day, and to the free society of the future, of which we are the pioneers, and which the "cause" represents. Furthermore, all ethical relations between individuals involve reciprocity —they imply a mutual obligation, a personal responsibility on either side. In the Middle Ages all relations in life were directly or indirectly personal in their character. The feudal relation was eminently a personal one. The mercantile relation, in so far as it existed, was a personal one. Now the sense of honour, honesty, etc., both logically and historically, has meaning alone in connection with a personal relation. Peter as an individual has certain definite moral relations to Paul, amongst others that of respecting his belongings, in so far as appropriation for personal use is concerned.* This is a relation as between man and man. He owes the obligation to Paul as a concrete individual, not to Paul's coat or his money. Paul, on the other hand, has identical obligations towards Peter. There is personal responsibility on either side. Again, the individual has plain duties towards the community, in so far as property designed for its use is concerned. (Of course, I am all along dealing with our present society.) He as an individual is bound to respect the belongings of the public; for instance, not to appropriate prints or books from the British Museum, not to destroy pictures in the National Gallery, not to steal commons or to "restore" ancient monuments (in which last two particulars, since they do not threaten the stability of Capitalism, the *bourgeois* conscience is more elastic than in the matter of "defrauding" companies) Here, also, the relation is between concretes —between a definite personality and a definite community. The pictures, books, commons, monuments are (or are supposed to be) there for the use and enjoyment of the community, and the community suffers a wrong in their destruction or alienation.

But to return to our Peter and Paul. We have said that the moral relation of Peter and Paul rests on a basis of reciprocal personal responsibility and on this alone. It was on such a basis that the feeling of honour in the dealings of life had its rise and in this alone it has any meaning. There was a relation of mutual personal obligation between the feudal lord and the vassal or serf. That the lord often neglected his obligation does not alter the fact of its existence. There was a personal relation between buyer and seller, master and workman, and indeed in every sphere of

* It is necessary to make this last *caveat*, as of course every Socialist will admit the justifiability of the community's confiscating individual wealth to public purposes, and of course any one individual might be the agent of this confiscation in any particular case.

life in the old time and in simpler conditions of
society. But with the rise of Capitalism the personal
relation has fallen into the background, personal
responsibility has been allowed to lapse to an ever-
increasing extent before the exigencies of modern
competitive conditions of industry. The responsible
proprietor of a business detaches himself more and
more as a personality from his business. The name
over the door may or may not be his own name, but
anyway he obliterates his personality as far as may be
by the addition of the words "& Co." You plead
with such a man for some act of grace to a creditor or
employé; "business is business," will be his reply,
a reply which surely enough indicates the impersonal,
anti-social methods of Commercialism. In pursuit of
its object, individual gain, Commercialism abstracts the
individual from his personality. The modern capitalist
lives a dual life; as *capitalist* he ceases more and
more to be *man*. Private relations and business relations tend to become more and more abstracted from
one another. Yet our capitalist forgets that it is only
as man, as a concrete personality, that he can justly
claim moral obligations from his fellow-men. If as the
"head of a firm" he stands in any moral relation to
other personalities, it is only by virtue of the fact that
the divorce between his manhood and his "headship
of the firm" is incomplete, that the personal relation
is not altogether abolished. His belongings as "head
of the firm" are to be respected, because even under
this disguise he is recognised as a thing of flesh and
blood.

But there is one form under which modern capitalism
functions—its most advanced form—in which the last
shred of personal responsibility is torn from its opera-
tions. We refer to what the French aptly call the
société anonyme—that thing without a name, the joint-
stock company. Here at last is naked capital, the last

shred of its human covering gone—capital without a capitalist—the thing of which the proverb says, it has " neither soul to save, nor heart to feel, nor body to kick." The abstraction is now complete, but at the same moment transformed into a hyperphysical, hyper-ethical entity. With the " head of the firm " there is always the chance (though possibly a faint one) that the man may get the better of the capitalist; human feelings may even hold back the demon " business "— the possibility of conscience is there to which to make your appeal. But here there is nothing but surplus-value. Fancy has imagined beings composed of water or of fire merely—Undines and Salamanders. Here is a being composed of the " circulating process of capital." By dint of the power of money the widow and orphan are ruined by litigation, are driven from court to court in search of their just and obvious claims. Employés of long-standing service are turned off at a week's notice when not wanted. You appeal to the conscience of the secretary, the manager, the director, against these enormities. The reply is simple: " We are here merely to look after the interests of the shareholders ;" which, being inter-preted, means, having duly appropriated the customary " pickings," to see that as much profit as possible is wrung out of " servants " and " public " regardless of all other considerations. But how about these share-holders ? Peter, let us say, is a shareholder. He is one of those who has *deliberately* merged a certain amount of his property (his belongings) in an im-personal abstraction, over the working of which he has practically no control. He has severed this portion of his belongings from his concrete individuality. It is a *quantum* of circulating capital abstracted from the man. The " company " consists entirely in a sum-total of such *quanta* of capital. The holder is merely an accident, both qualitatively and quantitatively. The

sum-total of these *quanta* of capital may be "held" in-
differently by twenty men or twenty thousand. They
may be clever or stupid, humane or criminal. As personalities they are utterly indifferent. Peter, though
a shareholder, is in his relation to the working of the
"company" but as one of the "ordinary public." The
member of a trade-firm, is personally responsible (more
or less) for the working of that firm. Not so here.
The man—the capitalist, if you will—has altogether
abstracted his "belongings" from that to which they
belong—from himself. It matters not what action
may be taken in the name of the "company," he, the
private shareholder, is powerless to prevent it. Once
in it, the ghastly Frankenstein may dance on his conscience, and beyond an impotent protest he can do
nothing. "But he can sell out," you will say. Of
what avails it? The action goes on; he has only
shifted the nominal responsibility from his own
shoulders to his neighbour's. The "company" remains. Holders come and holders go, but shares flow
on for ever. The company is constituted essentially
of the shares, and only accidentally of the men that
hold them.

In what relation, then, does the individual—concrete
man or woman—the thing of flesh and blood, stand to
this abstraction? We have taken for granted as indis-
putable, that we cannot stand in a moral relation to an
abstraction or an inanimate object or indeed to anything but a concrete sentient being. We cannot owe a
duty to Peter's coat or his money but only to Peter.
We cannot, therefore, stand in any *real* moral relation to
the joint-stock company. But the interests of Commercialism require that the wholly impersonal joint-
stock company, like the semi-personal business "firm,"
should be treated to all practical intents and purposes
as though it were a full living human personality. In
law, of course, it has the full rights of personality. In

morality it has stolen them, or tried to steal them. It claims (tacitly if not explicitly) in the name not only of law but of honour forsooth, a claim to make the gods laugh, respect for its " property " and the fulfilment of a bargain which it tacitly assumes the individual to be bound by when he takes advantage of the social function it casually performs (more or less badly) in pursuit of its sole end, the extraction of the greatest possible amount of *profit* from producer and consumer. The sacred name of " honour " and " honesty," origi- nating in far other conditions of society, and implying reciprocal obligations, is prostituted by the modern *bourgeois* mind to facilitate the "trickstering" and " profit-grinding " of modern competitive commerce for which on its own side moral obligations do not exist or exist at best on sufferance. But a suspicion of the instability of the title of the joint-stock company to be treated as a moral personality pierces the legal and conventional fiction A waft of healthy moral instinct whispers to a man that it is not the same thing to "defraud" a " company " as to rob his neighbour. But he does not know how to justify his instinctive im- pression. Hence when brought to book he cries a *mea culpa*. It is only the student of social evolution to whom the bogus nature of the title by which the "joint-stock " company, and to a lesser extent of that by which other forms of " commercial " individuality, impudently lay claim to recognition as object, of moral obligation, is revealed in all its clearness.

The " Slocum-Mudford railway company," let us suppose, appeals to the honour of the individual passenger not to prejudice its interests by " fraud " or otherwise. " But," says the individual, " who are you ? I as a moral man recognise my duty to all other persons individually as well as to the community as a whole. But you are neither an individual nor the community, and I decline to admit that I have any duties in your case at all. 'Peter I know, and Paul I know, but who are you?' My conscience does not respond to your appeal. It strikes me, on the contrary, that you and your congeners are fitting subjects for the free exercise of those free individualist tendencies about which the salaried defenders of the state of society which gives you birth, wax so eloquent. 'Business is business;' let us have no sentimentality. We are on a footing of competition, only that it is not 'free,' seeing that you have the law on your side. However, let that bide. Your 'business' is to get as much money-value as possible out of me the passenger on your line ('conveyance' being the specific form of social utility your capital works in, in order to realise itself as surplus value) and to give as little as possible in return, only in fact so much as will make your line pay. My 'business,' as an individual passenger, on the contrary, is to get as much use-value, to derive as much advantage from the social function which you casually perform in pursuance of your profit, as I possibly can, and to give you as little as possible in return. You seek under the protection of the law to guard yourself from 'fraud,' as you term it. Good. If I can evade the law passed in your interest and elude your vigilance, I have a perfect right to do so, and my success in doing so will be the reward of my ingenuity. If I fail I am only an unfortunate man The talk of 'dishonesty' or 'dishonour' where no moral obligation or 'duty' can possibly exist is absurd. You choose to make certain arbitrary rules to regulate the commercial game. I decline to pledge myself to be bound by them, and in so doing I am clearly within my moral right. We each try to get as much out of the other as we can, you in your way, I in mine. Only, I repeat, you are backed by the law, I am not. That is all the difference."

The question with which we set out has now been

answered. We took an extreme instance to start with, but our explanation covers the whole range of similar phenomena; for instance, the distinction felt between a "debt of honour" and a tradesman's bill. In the commercial relation as such the moral relation is abolished. In proportion as the personality, with its human responsibility, retreats into the background, leaving us confronted with the lifeless, bloodless vampire, Trade, by so much do the words "duty," "honour," morality," lose meaning. "Conscience," which has its ground in social union, can have no part nor lot with "Commerce," which has its ground in anti-social greed. But the transition from the personal or conscientious to the purely commercial relation is so gradual and is complicated by so many other factors, that it is quite easy for the *bourgeois* mind to keep up the fiction that honour or dishonour can be involved even in dealing with that commercial abstraction, the "joint-stock company." A general recognition of the sham claim of commercial abstractions to moral consideration, could not but prove embarrassing to the modern commercial system, which would then have to rely on its legal defences alone.

UNSCIENTIFIC SOCIALISM.

IN the exposition of a subject such as Socialism, as in the rebuilding of an edifice, there is a preliminary stage of destructive activity Old material, in the one case, has to be carted away, and the ground to be generally dug up and cleared. In the other, similarly, we have to clear out intellectual ground of theories likely to interfere with our contemplated structure. Now, no material is so much in danger of cumbering us as that which, though superficially resembling our own, is in reality old and rotten. In the following remarks I propose to examine briefly four codes of ideas (for theories or systems they cannot all of them be called) which are nominally socialistic, and profess certain principles in common with Socialism proper, but are, nevertheless, essentially distinct from it. These four codes of ideas are: I. Christian Socialism, so-called ; II. An indefinite kind of awakening to social imperfections among the youth of the middle classes to which I give the name *Sentimental Socialism;* III. The various social schemes propounded, and in part sought to be carried out in various parts of North America, dating from the earlier half of the nineteenth century, to which the general name of Utopian Socialism is commonly applied; IV. The doctrine or tendency generally known as Anarchism.

The Christian Socialism with which we are here concerned is not the imperial-Bismarckie device known by that name in Germany which to English readers, at least, is too transparent to need criticism, but a more insidious, because more honest attempt to pour new wine into old bottles. A body of High Churchmen, calling themselves the Guild of St. Matthew, held a series of meetings towards the close of the year 1883, for the discussion of this Christian Socialism. It was difficult to obtain any clear notion of what Christian Socialism meant from the ideas set forth by its professed exponents, setting aside the want of unanimity displayed. But to judge from most of the opening addresses, as well as from an explanatory letter published subsequently by the Rev. Canon Shuttleworth, what is understood as the practical basis of Christian Socialism, is trade co-operation or industrial partnership, such as has from time to time been carried out, and of which the Decorator's Co-operative Association is an example. This is significantly confirmed by the fact that the worthy canon, when asked at the close of his address in proof of an assertion he had made, to furnish the names of any socialist leaders who could, in any sense, be described as Christian—against the long array of anti-Christian names, from Marat and Babœuf to Lassalle and Marx, which were cited against him—could only bring forward those of the astute capitalist co-operators Leclaire and Godin, as historical evidence of the independent existence of the Christian Socialist. It was undoubtedly some scheme of private co-operation, we may also observe, that the "old original" Christian Socialists in this country, Kingsley and Maurice, had in view.

Now, a very little consideration suffices to show us that all such schemes are not only within the lines of the current *bourgeois* system of ideas, habits, and aspirations, but that they reflect that system in some of its worst aspects. As to the shrewd philanthropist Leclaire, the co-operator's "great man," verily he was not without his capitalistic reward, leaving, as he did, a fortune of £48,000 behind him. But personal questions apart, on entering one of these co-operative establishments what is the first thing that greets the eye? A list of "regulations," if anything more stringent than those of an ordinary workshop, indicating longer hours and harder work. The principle underlying these institutions, in fact, would seem to be that the supreme end of life is the maximisation of labour, and the minimisation of the enjoyment of its product. "Labour," or "industry" (as it would probably be termed), seems to be regarded by co-operators as one of those good things of which it is impossible to have too much. As a consequence they are jealous of all time spent otherwise than in labour, *i.e.*, manufacture of commodities, and are averse to the consumption or enjoyment of the product of such labour as at once a loss of time and a waste of material which would otherwise be saved. Now, all this may be very nice, but so far from being Socialism, it is the very antithesis of Socialism Trade co-operation is simply a form of industrial partnership, in which the society of co-operators is in the relation of capitalist to the outer world. The units of the society may be equal amongst themselves (always excepting the broken-down capitalist who is the presiding genius), but their very existence in this form presupposes exploitation going on above, below, and around them, in other words, the prevailing industrial anarchy.

As I have said, co-operative experiments reflect what are, from a Socialist point of view, the worst aspects of the current order. The trade co-operator canonises the *bourgeois* virtues, but socialist vices of "overwork," and "thrift." To the Socialist, labour is an evil to be minimised to the utmost The man who works at his trade or avocation more than necessity compels him, or who accumulates more than he can enjoy, is not a hero but a fool from the Socialist's standpoint. It is this necessary work which it is the aim of Socialism to reduce to the minimum. Again, " thrift," the hoarding up of the products of labour, it is obvious must be without rhyme or reason, except on a capitalist basis. For the only two purposes which commodities serve are consumption and exchange. Now, except under peculiar circumstances (Arctic expeditions and the like), it is certain they would not be " saved " to any considerable extent merely for the sake of future consumption. Hence the object of " thrift," or hoarding must lie in exchange. And it is indeed the increment obtainable by commodities or realised labour-power when represented by exchange-value or money that furnishes the only *raison d'être* of " thrift." The aim of the Socialist, therefore, which is the enjoyment of the products of labour as opposed to that of the *bourgeois* which is their mere accumulation with a view to profit in exchange is radically at variance with " thrift."

Having shown that in so far as it has any defined economic basis at all, " Christian Socialism " is anti-socialistic, it might seem hardly necessary to criticise it further ; but as a matter of fact the whole scheme is so vague and intangible, that it is quite possible some persons may really believe in the accomplishment of vast changes (whether the *modus operandi* be the expropriation of competition rents, or what not) of a really socialistic nature mainly through the instrumentality of a clarified Christianity,—a Christianity which shall consist apparently of the skins of dead dogmas stuffed with an adulterated socialist ethics, and of formulas which, though to the simple mind they seem plain enough, the brotherhood of the Guild of St. Matthew will show us mean something quite different from what they seem.

In justice it must be said that the ritualistic priests we are here criticising exhibit a generosity and a charity which they may call Christian, but which seem to us very much better than anything in the way of those commodities we have seen produced by Christianity outside the Guild of St. Matthew. There is only one thing that appears to ruffle the usually equable temper of these gentlemen, and that is, to be confronted with any definite dogma, text, or formula. Not that we have ever found them at a loss to explain away the irrational and immoral in such into something perfectly harmless, rational, moral, and worthy of all acceptation, when called upon to do so; but they, nevertheless, appear to think such things as recognised Christian doctrines quite irrelevant even when the possibility of such a combination as Christian Socialism is in question. Our Neo-Christian friends may, without any special inconsistency, refuse to be saddled with "Semitic myths," or may even contend, as did Canon Shuttleworth, that the Christianity they profess is independent of the Canonical Hebrew Scriptures considered as a whole. But surely they at least must be prepared to stand by the accepted character and teaching of their titular founder. It is surely fair to confront them with this. Now it is upon the ground of this traditional character and teaching that we are prepared to join issue with them when they assert its Socialistic nature. We can readily understand the charm it exercises on certain minds. We know that inherited tendencies, upbringing and the like, all conduce in sensitive natures to clothe with the rich and glowing hues of their own beauty and emotion a shadowy figure, in which those who have divested themselves of those tendencies, and view things with the colder eye of impartiality, see at best a weak but impulsive personality. But it is only natural that these latter should resent with some indignation the continual reference of ideal perfection to a semi-mythical Syrian of the first century, when they see higher types even in some now walking this upper earth, but in vulgar flesh and blood, and without

the atmosphere of nineteen centuries to lend enchant-
ment to them. How many such are there not and
have there not been in the modern socialist movement
who do their work, give up their all, without posing as
Messiahs, but choosing rather the nobler part of sinking
their individuality in their cause?

As to the ethical teaching of Christ with its one-sided,
introspective, and individualistic character, we venture
to assert that no one acquainted with the theory of
modern scientific Socialism can for one moment call it
socialistic. Socialism aims rather at a rehabilitation
(in a higher form) of the classical utilitarian morality
of public life. It has no sympathy with the morbid,
eternally-revolving-in-upon-itself transcendent morality
of the Gospel discourses. This morality, like that of
the whole Oriental movement of which it is a development, is essentially subjective, its criterion lying in
the individual conscience, and its relation to a divinity
supposed to reveal himself in it. It sets up a forced,
to the vast majority impossible standard of "personal
holiness," which, when realised, has seldom resulted in
anything but (1) an apotheosised priggism (*e.g.*, the
Puritan type), or (2) in an epileptic hysteria (*e.g.*, the
Catholic saint type), and which at the best is a *tour
de force* involving an amount of concentrated moral
energy that may excite our wonder perhaps, like the
concentrated physical energy of the tight-rope dancer,
but which we feel to be just as useless. But if it is
useless in those exceptional cases where attained, it is
worse than useless in its effects on the generality of
men. With Christian asceticism as the ethical standard
which all good men are supposed to attain, but which
as a matter of fact hardly any good man really thinks of
attaining, men are driven to the compromise of pretend-
ing to attain it. It is thus that hypocrisy arises. In
the classical world hypocrisy was virtually unknown.
Aristotle, in his elaborate analysis of virtues and vices

in the Nich. Ethics, barely alludes to it.   It was born of
the Oriental-introspective ethics of Christianism, and
with their establishment in Europe it took its place as an
integral factor of social life.   This has been more than
ever the case since the triumph of its most purely
individualist form—Protestantism.   The success of
Christianity as a moral force has been solely upon
isolated individuals.   In its effect on societies at large
it has signally and necessarily failed.   Though Socialism
has no sympathy with anti-Semitism as generally
understood, it certainly represents the reassertion of
the typical Aryan ethics (whether classical or Norse)
of social utility as against the typical Semitic ethics
of personal holiness.   (I say the Semitic ethics
since the so-called Christian ethics were no more the
discovery of Jesus than of Hillel, of Philo, or of any
other individual, but like all great movements and
discoveries, were the result of the concentrated thought
of generations.)

The brotherhood of the Guild of St. Matthew merely
represents a phase common to ages of transition in
which the reactionary ideal and morality endeavours to
steal a march on the progressive ideal and morality.
The modern Broad-High Church, or eclectic movement
in Christendom offers an exact analogy to the eclectic
movement in Paganism of the third and fourth centuries
A.D.   In either, a *modus vivendi* is sought to be effected
between the immorality and absurdity of the popular
theology, Pagan or Christian, and the growing aspirations of the earnest and thoughtful.   And the manner
in which this is done is no less analogous.   The whole
external structure of dogma, legend, and ceremonial is
retained, not a tittle of it is repudiated, while it is
carefully emptied of all its original and obvious
meaning, and by a dexterous ingenuity is forced to
mean something which neither " Christian, Pagan, nor
man " ever dreamt of its meaning before.

An attempt at mutilating or defacing the exterior of
a creed or cultus is always unsuccessful. The purification of Paganism sought to be effected by the Epi-
cureans and earlier Platonists through the rejection of
the legends of the poets and popular traditions respecting the gods, and the shearing down of ceremonial,
touched only a section of the cultured. The only
clarified Paganism, even temporarily successful, was that
represented by Plotinus, Porphyry, Julian, and Proclus,
which held every legend and ceremonial sacred, while
reading into them the Oriental ethics then becoming
popular. Similarly, the barren ceremonial and un-
symmetrical theology of Unitarianism has never had
any success save among a limited section of the middle
classes. Taking these facts into consideration, to wit,
that symmetry of creed and taste in ritual count for
much in human nature and in the popularity of a
cultus, the move made by the Guild of St. Matthew
and similar associations is strategically not a bad one
from the standpoint of clericalism. But its achieve-
ment of even the temporary success of the Neo-
Platonists (which was owing in great measure to causes
not now in operation) is more than doubtful. The
working-classes see plainly enough that Christianity in
all its forms belongs to the world of the past and the
present, but not to that world of the future which
signifies their emancipation.

The sentimental Socialist, though not necessarily
Christian, retains essentially the introspective attitude
of the Christian ethics. He forms societies, the members of which are supposed to pledge themselves to
indefinitely high aims,—aims that tower above the
clouds from which it requires the practised eye to
distinguish them. These aims " won from the void
and formless infinite," seem to be only won for the
sake of being handed over to the equally formless
indefinite. The only shape approaching articulation

into which they wreathe themselves, is that of resolutions and letters. The young people of the well-to-do
middle-class, for whom sentimental Socialism possesses
attractions, think human nature susceptible of higher
aims than the current ones, and meet in drawing-
rooms for the apparent purpose of passing resolutions
to that effect. The sentimental Socialist desires above
all things to be broad and comprehensive. Now any
proposition conveying a distinct meaning is necessarily
limited by that meaning, and must be taken to exclude
its opposite, and *à fortiori* the society adopting it to
exclude those who hold its opposite. But how can a
society whose aims are so high condescend to such
matters of detail as *meaning*? How can a man as
catholic as the "Brother of the Higher Life," or a
member of the "Communion of Noble Aspirations,"
or of the "New Atlantis Society" be so narrow as to
exclude any one. Hence in the resolutions adopted by
such associations, the first requisite is the absence of
meaning. All is possible in the man (or woman) who
aims high enough. Danton's motto "To dare, to dare,
and again to dare," becomes in the hands of the
Sentimental Socialist, "To aim, to aim, and again to
aim" at an ineffable O—*Voilà tout*. All this "casting
of empty buckets into empty wells and drawing nothing
up," may be entertaining, beautiful, ennobling for
a short spell, but palls after a time, which is probably
the explanation of the fact that these societies that
start so rosy bright invariably die of inanition within
measurable distance of their inauguration though
only to make way for new ones. The young men
and women of our *blasé* middle-class civilisation require
a stimulus; this stimulus may be æsthetic, philan-
thropic, or social. It may consist in languishing
vapouring on art, on improved dwellings, on social
reconstruction. Just now it wears the latter aspect.
The whole movement is born of the morbid self-

consciousness of our Christian and middle-class civilisation run to seed.

The Utopian Socialist schemes of the first half of the present century, which are conveniently brought forward by the votaries of the current *bourgeois* economy as a dummy to be battered down, under the pretence of demolishing Socialism proper, stand condemned *ab initio*, owing to their lack of a scientific basis. These attempts bear the same relation to modern scientific Socialism that astrology and alchemy do to astronomy and chemistry. The attempt of Goethe's Wagner to construct a homunculus artificially was scarcely more preposterous than the attempt of Owen, Fourier, or St. Simon to construct a society artificially. It is as rational to introduce Owen, Fourier, etc., with their " New Harmonies " and " phalansteries," into discussions on scientific Socialism, as it would be to introduce Paracelsus or Van Helmont, with their *bains de marie* and their "marriages" of metals into discussions on chemistry. Utopian Socialism was only the prescientific and infantile stage of that matured science of society which modern Socialism represents on its practical side. Yet there are people who even still believe in (more or less) select little bands going into the backwoods and founding colonies, undeterred by the numberless wrecks of shattered hopes they see around them. No experiment of this kind, as might be expected, has had (even avowedly) any other than a Christian or sentimental basis. Most of the so-called communistic societies of the United States are really nothing more than religious sects, which have found it convenient to come out of the world. They have really no more right to the special appellation " socialist " than a body of monks.

Of course, in a sense, any monastic society may be termed communistic, inasmuch as its members practise, like the early Christians or the Essenes, a certain

primitive communism or community of goods. And
in this sense of course the erratic Protestant sects of
the United States—the Shakers, the Perfectionists,
the Separatists, etc.—who have formed themselves into
similar independent communities on a somewhat larger
scale, may be termed communistic or socialistic. Otherwise the term Socialist has no meaning as applied to
them—least of all in the modern scientific sense of
the word in which Socialism is conceived of as the
result of a transformation of the existent conditions of
society throughout the civilised world, and to which,
therefore, any " coming out of the world," in the sense
of establishing an independent " community of saints,"
is an anachronism. Socialism proper presupposes the
developed industrial system, the machinery, the population, etc., of the most advanced countries of modern
times as its essential antecedent condition, and whether
right or wrong, true or false, takes its stand on the continuity of historic evolution. It is no Utopian scheme
or theory of what a model society might be, but claims
to be a deduction as to what the outcome of our present
capitalistic civilisation itself *must* be sooner or later,
unless social evolution is to be arrested by dissolution.
(Political economists who interpolate chapters on
" Communism " or " Socialism " into their treatises,
please take note.)

The last point referred to brings us to the question
of Anarchism. Now the Anarchist frankly accepts the
alternative of dissolution. He desires no reorganisation.
He is a logical, thorough-going individualist—none of
your sham *bourgeois* individualists, whose conception
of individual liberty is the liberty of themselves and
their class to "exploit" those below them without
restriction, under the guise of freedom of contract—
but an individualist whose conceptions of individual
liberty is absolute for each and all, and knows no distinction. The Anarchist would resolutely destroy all

organisation whatever, however salutary. He would resolve society into its component units—in other words, as we said, his goal is social dissolution. Every bond of social union would be severed, each individual free to make a "little hell" for himself. Our first criticism on this is that disintegration such as the Anarchist aims at, even if brought about, could hardly endure for a day. The social organism in its present stage is analogous to those low biological organisms which, subdivide as you will, recombine and reorganise by their very nature and that of the medium in which they exist. The result of any violent disintegration, if successful, that is, if the whole of the middle-class civilisation of to-day were entirely *destroyed*—rather than *transformed* or *changed* into a new and higher social state, which is what the Collectivist aims at—would simply recombine on lines belonging to a lower stage of the old economic development; the old society wold *reform*, but at the point arrived at fifty years ago or more, and the whole intervening period, or something similar, would have to be gone over again. This is the utmost that would be achieved. The social organism is, as yet, in too low a stage to be more than temporarily deranged in its development by any violence that could be done it. A violent dissolution—were this possible, a point we do not argue,—would be speedily followed by redintegration on the old lines.

We have, of course, merely referred to the possibility of the permanence of Anarchism, and have said nothing as to the desirability of the destruction of those elements of the current civilisation, brought by the bitter toil and experience of centuries of human effort, which, though under the present organisation of society, they merely serve for the enslavement of the greater portion of mankind, under a higher organisation might be the means of their emancipation from the bondage of toil, and of affording the possibility of

comfort, art, and culture for each and all. The struggle
between man and nature — including that which is
natural, *i.e.*, merely animal and brutal in man—can
with certainty only be maintained to the advantage of
the former by organisation and to us it seems that
Anarchism stands self-condemned when once these facts
are clearly seen.* At the same time, it is only fair to
remember that the Anarchist does *not* see this, to most
thinkers, obvious truth. His goal and that of the collectivist is similar substantially. But the collectivist
would take the sure historic highway of organisation
to that Liberty, Equality, and Fraternity which the
Anarchist would seek in vain to reach by the abrupt
but suicidal plunge of dissolution. It must not be
supposed from what is here said that we favour the
orthodox prejudice as to the ineffectiveness of violent
revolutions as such. On the contrary, we recognise the
teaching of history that no great change has ever taken
place without a convulsion or series of convulsions, and
we do not believe that the transformation of material
conditions which lies before us will be accomplished
without some such struggle.

But every world-historic idea contains within it an
immanent contradiction, which becomes explicit as it
progresses towards realisation. The Socialist idea has
a *de*structive and a *con*structive side. The appearance
of these two sides in abstraction and mutual opposition
causes the mere *form* of the process of change to be
mistaken for the end itself. An antagonism is thus
evoked in which we have on the one side Anarchism,
the mere apotheosis of destruction, and on the other, a
parliamentary or State-collectivism, with a tendency to
eliminate the revolutionary element essential to the
realisation of the idea in the concrete. True Socialism

---

* It should be stated that the above criticism applies only in a
modified degree, to the (so-called) Communist-Anarchist section of
the party.

recognises that force is the midwife of progress, though not the end, yet an essential means.

Of the unscientific Socialist standpoints we have passed in review the most important, numerically and influentially (more especially, as it has the credit on the Continent of being the most revolutionary party), is the Anarchist. The least so, inasmuch as it is confined to this country, and to a small body of priests and a limited section of the English middle class, is that of the Christian and Sentimental Socialists respectively. Our reason for devoting so much space to these latter was the desirability in view of the English public of exposing any "red-herring" which might retard, however slightly or temporarily, the genuine Socialist movement now beginning in England. Utopian Socialism used as a convenient "aunt Sally" by Political Economists, who know all the time it is not genuine Socialism they are expounding or attacking, is certainly an irritating, but scarcely a dangerous phenomenon from a practical point of view; while Anarchism, pure and simple, can hardly be said to count a "party" in this country. There is probably more danger in Great Britain in a Conservative "red-herring" than in a (so-called) "advanced" one, such as Anarchism. With Mr. Henry George we have not dealt, inasmuch as land nationalisation is the child of true Socialism, though it has been by Mr. George "untimely ripped from its mother's womb." Land communisation can only come effectively as the natural issue of a general Socialist revolution. When torn from this connection it can but be abortive

THE CRIMINAL COURT JUDGE.

THE occupant of the judicial bench is, as we all know, the functionary selected by the governmental "ring," to enforce or put into action the cumbrous machinery of law, which the civilised world has been compelled to invent as a feeble corrective to the results of its civilisation. We have spoken of the governmental "ring," but we might more accurately describe a modern state-bureaucracy as a system of "rings," interlacing one within the other. Each "department" has its traditions carefully kept up by its staff of permanent officialdom. The "bosses" of these departments, that is, of the central or ministerial ring (and for that matter the others also), emanate, of course, from "society" as it is termed, that is, from the aristocratic and plutocratic cliques of the West End; but what is more, under our system of party government a particular ministerial post is generally the exclusive appanage of two or three individuals who take it in turns and then begin again. The appointment and regulation of the judicial bench rests respectively with the Lord Chancellor and the Home Secretary. It is true the powers of these worthies are practically limited by the "traditions" of the subordinate judicial "ring" itself (a brotherhood as jealous of its privileges and dignity as the Corporation of London, or any other mutual benefit society), but appointments, revision of sentences, and general supervision rest in the last resort with the dignitaries in question. The Lord Chancellor, for the most part, appoints the judge from a successful barrister with "influential" connections.

Now, our object in thus exposing in a few words the mechanism of our constitutional government in general, and its relation to the judicial system in particular, is the better to grasp the nature of the semi-divinity which with the public at large seems to hedge a judge and all his utterances. The juryman obediently follows his directions as to the verdict he shall return; in fact, in many instances juries would seem to regard it as the sole reason of their being, to please the presiding judge and give glory to him. The public in court, and the public out of court, hang upon the pronouncement from the bench as placing beyond question the enormity of the guilt of the luckless victim (it may be) of judicial rancour. How is this reverence for the judicial fiat to be accounted for? Doubtless, to a large extent, it has its origin like the divine right of kings, and many other things, in a state of society where the judicial authority was also the religious and civil head of the community—in short, that it is one of those numerous sentiments which had a meaning once, in bygone stages of human society and intelligence, but which have survived their meaning and lapsed into superstitions. But it is, in fact, only one instance of that respect for law and order in the average mind on which the stability of the *bourgeois* state rests, and which masks the true character of the latter as the prop of economical rottenness.

Let us consider for a moment what judgeship involves. We have every day illustrations of the fact that the judicial "ring" presumes upon the respect accorded it, so there can be no doubt that if the people could be induced to see the judge in the light merely of an overpaid servant of the modern state, who absorbs an enormous proportion of their earnings, the better would it be for the soul's welfare of the judicial bench

itself, as well as for the cause of fairplay. Paradox
as it may seem, it is an undoubted truth that no judge
can be strictly an honest man. The judge must
necessarily be a man of inferior moral calibre. Though
it is a thing one would say of no other man or body of
men, yet I say unhesitatingly that a judge by the fact
of his being a judge proclaims himself a creature on a
lower moral level than us ordinary mortals, and this
without any assumption of moral superiority above the
average on our part. And why? Because the aspiring
member of the bar when he accepts a judgeship knows
that in so doing he *deliberately pledges himself* to
functions which may at any moment compel him to act
against his conscience and wrong another man. He
deliberately pledges himself, that is, to be false to himself. He may any day have to pass sentence on one
whom he believes to be innocent. He lays himself
under the obligation of administering a law which he
may know to be bad on any occasion when called upon,
merely because it is a law. He makes this surrender
of humanity and honour for what? For filthy lucre
and tawdry notoriety. Now, I ask, can we conceive a
more abjectly contemptible character than that which
acts thus? If we want further proof of the utter
degeneracy of moral tissue in such a being, let us examine the sophistries he uses in his defence, and which
he endeavours on occasion to force down the throat of
the recalcitrant juryman. He does not make the law,
he will tell you, he merely administers it. In the
same way Bill Sykes does not make his jemmy and
other burglarious implements, he merely administers
them. This is the sort of oil he pours on his uneasy
conscience when he has one. The juryman disapprov-
ing of capital punishment objects to convicting a
murderer. He is told he has nothing to do with the
sentence, but only with the evidence; in other words,
that the fact that the verdict he gives will have for its

direct consequence a result he regards with abhorrence, is to count for nothing with him. Men who can willingly *pretend*—I say *pretend*, since it must be remembered we are dealing with men of ability and culture, capable of exposing many a subtler fallacy when it suits them—men who can *pretend* to accept such flimsy trash as cogent argument must surely be dead to all respect for honesty.

But the festering mass of hypocrisy of which bench-dom consists is only too evident at every turn. There is, of course, the hypocrisy which is racy of the judicial soil, just as there is the hypocrisy which is racy of the clerical soil. To this belongs the professed deep rever-ence for the "law of England," when no one knows better than the benchman who has studied it, that well-nigh one half of English law is based on effete super-stition, of which it presents in many cases the most grotesque instances—interesting and instructive from a historical point of view, doubtless, but not in them-selves calculated to awaken feelings of reverence in the modern mind—and that the other half is founded on the baldest class interest and prejudice. So that all things considered there is hardly a branch of learning the pursuit of which is more calculated to inspire the average student with a contempt for its subject-matter than English law—hardly even excepting Divinity. But what is more offensive than this is the impudent assumption of moral superiority, which is one of the "properties" of the profession. Quite apart from any of the considerations just adduced, it is perfectly well known that there are among members of the English bench men of a deb——, well, men that enjoy life on its animal side, as is, indeed, only natural, considering the amount of time and money on their hands. Yet who can orate with a richer profusion of impressively delivered platitudes drawn from the current morality than the *puisne* in addressing the prisoner, who has

in ninety-nine cases out of a hundred, brought himself
within reach of the law by the desire to obtain some
of those very pleasures in which the judge himself
revels. It is scarcely to be expected but that a man
who in a "higher" grade of society so-called is capable
of accepting a judgeship (with its conditions as described above) would not in a "lower," where the
temptations were of a different order and much more
severe, be capable of doing a little housebreaking,
forgery, or even bigamy or rape. Such being the case
the elimination from judicial proceedings of the "John
Jacob Jackson, you have been convicted on the clearest
evidence of, etc. . . . To remonstrate with such a man
as you would be useless, etc., etc.," with the epilogue,
"I should be failing in my duty if I did not pass a heavy
sentence," etc.—the elimination, I say, then, of this
somewhat stale "gag" from judicial proceedings, might
possibly have a tendency to keep alive respect for law
somewhat longer than bids fair otherwise to be the case.

In France even middle-class public opinion has had
to assent to the abolition of the scandal of the judge's
summing-up, but respect for law and order is too great
in this country to allow of this instalment of justice
towards accused persons. But, surely, even in this
country, a muzzle might be applied to the judge after
the verdict. If Parliament were to employ itself in
doing this it would at least prevent unoffending citizens
being sickened by the nauseous rant which on the
occasion of every important trial now emanates from
the whited sepulchre in wig and gown, whose function
it is to administer the law.

That society which is based on property and privilege
must have a criminal code as its necessary consequence
we are well aware, but we none the less protest against
its "administrator," the judge, being regarded in any
more honourable light than its other "administrator,"
the hangman.

SOME BOURGEOIS IDOLS; OR IDEALS, REALS, AND SHAMS.

THERE are certain catchwords which have a marvellous charm to calm the breast political, a magic power to levitate the mind captivated by them, out of the regions of mere argument and recognition of facts. Such a hold do these words and the deified abstractions they cover have on the average man of the nineteenth century, that they and they alone are worshipped as the ultimate manifestation of goodness, beauty, and truth. To be opposed to these abstractions is to be condemned as blasphemous against the first principles of rectitude, moral and political.

Let us take Liberty. What a charming phrase that is, what a word to conjure with! What a thrill can be evoked from an average audience by the tub-thumper who waves his hand and pronounces the magic formula "liberty of conscience" or "liberty of contract." Little recks the applauding *bourgeois* whether he has the living reality itself, or merely the empty hull from which the soul has long since fled. Little recks he whether the thing he clasps be human or not. Liberty as expressed in Liberty of contract, of conscience, etc., as understood by the *bourgeois* of to-day, has been dead wellnigh this three centuries and buried since the French Revolution ; the shibboleth that now stalks in its semblance is its vampire, and, like other vampires, it has but one function, to suck the life-blood from its living kin—real liberty.

Time was when our modern "liberty of contract" was the expression of a living reality. Feudal oppression said in effect to the labourer, "You shall only work for one master, for him who is your lord, under whom you were born; you shall work for him for ever, even though he be unjust, harsh, or cruel, and you shall render him his accustomed dues whatever they may be." As against this principle of traditional *status* the rising *bourgeois* world invoked "liberty of contract." "Liberty of contract" was then a reality as against its negation, the tyranny of *status*. The victory of *contract* over *status* having been once definitively assured, one might have imagined that liberty was thereby assured also. And this is what the *bourgeois* thought and thinks still. He will not recognise the subtle change that has come over "liberty of contract" in the moment of its supremacy—that the tyranny to which it opposed itself is now absorbed into itself. So long as the barren form is there, it matters not to him that by means of the modern revolution in the conditions of production and distribution, its content, its living principle is no longer what it was, but the opposite of what it was—that the body of liberty is animated by the soul of slavery. Hence the horror of the ordinary Radical at the sacrilegious hand that would boldly transfix the vampire-body, notwithstanding the honoured shape it bears. He feels the blow struck at liberty of contract is a blow struck at himself, at the core of his being. And in this he is surely not unreasonable. For is he not himself the embodiment of a contract-system? What *bourgeois* sentiment really cares for and has cared for, in its revolt against *status*, is not liberty, but the development of the *bourgeois* world. "Liberty of contract" was essential to this development in its war with *status*, and, therefore, received honour at its hands, not because of *liberty*, but because of *contract*—the power of contract being

its only means of realisation. Liberty is the bait held
out to the proletarian fish covering the hook of contract. Unless labour can be contracted for, *i.e.*, caught
by the capitalist, it is of no more use to him than
the fish that remain in the sea are to the fisherman.
"Liberty" in the sense of the orthodox economist is,
then, in brief, an empty abstraction which stands in
flagrant antagonism to the real, the concrete liberty of
the Socialist. The abstract liberty of the economist is
the liberty to die quickly of starvation or slowly of the
same. The Socialist knows no such liberty as this.
He cares not for the liberty to change masters with
identical conditions in either case ; he cares not for the
liberty to refuse work and starve quickly or accept it
and starve slowly. He would be glad to see such
liberty for ever abolished. The liberty he values is
the concrete liberty for individuality to assert itself,
the leisure or freedom from work and care which is
essential thereto, and which, with comfortable circumstances and good surroundings, make up the *sine quâ
non* of all real liberty. Thus the "liberty" which to
the mind of the latter Middle Ages was an ideal, and
which became a real in the earlier phases of the
modern world, has evaporated to a sham in the world of
to-day.

"Liberty of conscience" is, again, another of the
glib phrases so neatly rolled off the tongue, and which
are supposed to crush an opponent against whom they
are invoked by their mere intrinsic weight. This, too,
as employed by the ordinary Freethinker and Radical,
is often but a vampire, a semblance of a reality which
has ceased to be. The typical British "Freethinker"
would regard with horror as a violation of that sacred
idol "liberty of conscience," any attempt under any
circumstances to prevent the infusion into minds incapable of judgment of doctrines which he would
admit to be injurious morally and perhaps even

8

physically. His sheet-anchor is argument and reasonable persuasion. But let us take a case. A child or
person intellectually incapable either naturally or
through ignorance or both, comes under the influence
of the Salvation Army or the worst kind of Catholic
priest, it matters not which, is terrified by threats of
the wrath of God into " conversion," becomes the slave
of General Booth or the " Church," is warped morally
and mentally for life, and in the worst case possibly
driven to religious mania. There's the result of liberty
of conscience! The *bourgeois* Freethinker, hide-bound
in this abstraction, is quite oblivious of the fact that,
though the form of liberty is there, it does but
enshrine the reality of slavery; that it is a liberty to
deprive others of liberty. It would be intolerance,
forsooth, to suppress the Salvation Army, he will tell
you; liberty of conscience demands that the Salvation
Army and every other body or individual shall have
the privilege of enslaving the minds of the young or
the ignorant by threats or cajolery, of fooling them to
the top of their bent. Against this the only weapon
he permits himself is argument or persuasion. He
forgets that argument is only a reliable weapon when
employed against argument, *i.e.*, against a doctrine
avowedly based on reason, and that against one which
makes its appeal, not to reason, but to faith, fear, and
ignorance, argumentative persuasion must be a broken
reed. The freedom to hold and propound any proposition, however absurd, as a theory to be judged of, and
accepted or rejected at the bar of Reason, is quite
another thing from the liberty of the " hot gospeller,"
who claims to hold a speculative pistol to the ear of
ignorant and weak-minded people by threatening them
with damnation if they reject his teaching. The one
is of the essence of real liberty, the other is the
vampire of a dead liberty of conscience which was only
living and real when it was opposed to the positive

power of the representatives of dogma over men's persons and lives. As Gabriel Deville well puts it, " The aim of collectivity is to assure liberty to each, understanding by this the means of self-development and action, since there can be no liberty where there is the material or moral incapacity of consciously exercising the faculty of will. . . . To permit by religious practices the cerebral deformation of children is in reality a monstrous violation of liberty of conscience, which can only become effective after the proscription of what at present passes muster for religious liberty, the odious licence in favour of some to the detriment of all." The vampire, *bourgeois* liberty of conscience, must in short be impaled, before true liberty of conscience can become a healthy living reality.

Let us take another idol. This time we tread on sacred ground indeed—equality between the sexes. Well may the iconoclastic hand tremble before levelling a blow at this new Serapis. Nevertheless here also—as the phrase is understood by the ordinary modern woman's right advocate—we are bound to recognise a vampire. In earlier stages of social development, woman was placed in a condition of undoubted social inferiority to man. Into the grounds of this inferiority it is unnecessary here to enter. Suffice it to say it existed, and that against the state of things it implied the cry of " equality between the sexes" was raised, at first in a veiled, and afterwards in an open manner. For some time it represented a real tendency towards equality by the removal of certain undoubted grievances. But for some time past the tendency of the *bourgeois* world, as expressed in its legislation and sentiment, has been towards a factitious exaltation of the woman at the expense of the man—in other words, the cry for " equality between the sexes " has in the course of its realisation become a sham, masking a *de facto* inequality. The inequality in

question presses, as usual, heaviest upon the working-
man, whose wife, to all intents and purposes, now has
him completely in her power. If dissolute or drunken,
she can sell up his goods or break up his home at
pleasure, and still compel him to keep her and live
with her to her life's end. There is no law to protect
him. On the other hand, let him but raise a finger in
a moment of exasperation against this precious representative of the sacred principle of " womanhood," and
straightway he is consigned to the treadmill for his six
months amid the jubilation of the *D. T.* and its
kindred, who pronounce him a brute and sing pæans
over the power of the " law" to protect the innocent
and helpless female. Thus does *bourgeois* society
offer sacrifice to the idol " equality between the sexes."
For the law jealously guards the earnings or property of
the *wife* from possible spoliation. She on any colour-
able pretext can obtain magisterial separation and
" protection."

Again, we have the same principle illustrated in the
truly bestial outcry raised every now and again by
certain persons for the infliction of the punishment
of flogging on *men* for particular offences, notably
" assaults on women and children." As a matter of
fact, in the worst cases of cruelty to children, women
are the offenders. Some few months back there was
a horrible instance in which a little girl was done to
death by a stepmother in circumstances of the most loath-
some barbarity ; yet these horror-stricken apostles of the
lash never venture to support flogging as a wholesome
corrective to viragos of this description. It would be
opposed to middle-class sentiment, which would regard
such a proposition as blasphemy against the sacred
principle of " femality." No other explanation is
possible, since it can hardly be assumed that even the
bourgeois mind is incapable of grasping the obvious
fact that a man pinioned and in the hands of half a

dozen prison-warders, is in precisely as helpless a
condition as any woman in a like case, and that, therefore, the brutality or cowardice of the proceeding is
no greater in the one case than in the other. The
bourgeois conception of "equality between the sexes"
is aptly embodied in that infamous clause of the
"Criminal Law Amendment Act," which provides that
in case of illicit intercourse between a boy and girl
under sixteen years of age, though the girl escapes scot
free, the boy is liable to five years' imprisonment in a
reformatory.

Even the great Radical nostrum which is supposed
to involve the quintessence of political equality, is,
when closely viewed, the hollowest of shams. The
revolutionary Socialist perhaps does not much concern
himself about questions of the suffrage, esteeming
but lightly the privilege of electing men to help to
carry on the present system of society, which he
believes destined to perish before long. But looked at
from the ordinary point of view, it is quite clear that
considering the fact that the female population of
England is in excess of the male by about a million,
female suffrage, in spite of its apparent embodiment of
the principle of equality, really means, if it means
anything at all (which may be doubtful) the handing
over of the complete control of the state to *one* sex.
These are only a few of the illustrations, which might
be multiplied almost indefinitely, of the truth that the
tendency of the modern middle-class world, is, while
proclaiming the principle of "equality between the
sexes" in opposition to the feudal subjection of woman,
to erect the female sex into a quasi-privileged class.
The real equality between the sexes aimed at by
Socialism is as much opposed to this Brummagem
sentiment and sham equality, as it is to the female-
slavery of ancient times, of which, of course, we do not
wish to deny that survivals remain even at the present

day. With the economic emancipation of woman and
the gradual transformation of the state-system of to-day
into an international league of free communes, the
feudal subjection of women to man and the middle-
class subjection of man to woman will be alike at an
end.

Yet another *bourgeois* idol—the rights of majorities.
The Radical mind, instead of placing before it the
concrete ideal—Human Happiness,—erects an abstract
idol in its room as the supreme end of all endeavour.
The Radical's first question is not, does such or such
a course conflict with social well-being, but does it not
violate one of our supreme dogmas? There is no more
frequent charge brought against the revolutionary
Socialist than that of despotic interference with the
right of the majority. Socialism, it is indeed true, in
pursuit of its central purpose, treats with scant reverence
the household gods of the Radical. The abstract
principle of the right of the majority is of as small
concern to the Socialist as the equally abstract
principle of "liberty of contract" or "liberty of
conscience." And why? Because, like the rest, the
bourgeois "right of the majority" is the vampire of
a dead reality. Feudalism, and the centralising
monarchical tendency which succeeded feudalism
proper, opposed the will of the feudal few or of
the monarchical one to the will of the majority of
propertied persons, *i.e.*, the rising middle class. The
ascendency of this rising middle class then represented
the extent of popular aspiration. The decaying
principle was Feudalism and the monarchical Absolu-
tism it left behind it. As against the privilege and
traditional *status* upon which this based itself, Liberalism asserted as its ideal the right of the majority of
the people as then understood—*i.e.*, of the middle
classes—to self-government. Hard upon the realisation
of this ideal has followed its reduction to sham. Con-

ditions are changed in the Western Europe of to-day.
With the entrance upon the arena of the modern
proletariat of capitalism and the differentiation of class-
interests therein involved, the old popular sovereignty
has become a meaningless phrase. The old majority
has ceased to be the majority, has become a minority,
and the new majority is in the thraldom of this
minority (the franchise notwithstanding). Capitalist
fraud has succeeded to feudal force ; the castle has
given place to the factory.

The new majority, consisting of the proletariat and
all those who suffer from the present system, are in
the thrall of Capitalism. With no leisure for thought
or education, they are necessarily the victims of every
sophism of middle-class economists and politicians,
even where they are not directly coerced or cajoled
by their masters. The majority know that they suffer,
they know that they want not to suffer, but they know
not *why* they suffer, and they know not *how* they may
cease to suffer. The majority, therefore, under a
capitalist system will necessarily for the most part
vote for the maintenance of that system under one
guise or another, not because they love it, but out of
sheer ignorance and stupidity. It is by the active
minority from out the stagnant inert mass that the
revolution will be accomplished. It is to this Socialist
minority that individuals, acting during the revolutionary period, are alone accountable. The Socialist
leader or delegate, as such, does not take account of
the absolute majority of the population, which consists
of two sections—*i.e.*, of those who are interested in the
maintenance of the present system and those who are
blind or inert enough to be misled by them. To
disregard the opinion (if such it can be called) of these
latter is no more tyranny than it is tyranny to hold a
drunken man back by force when he seeks to get out
of the door of a railway carriage with the train going

at full speed. The man does not want to be maimed or killed; he is simply misled by his drunken fancy as to what is conducive to his welfare. In the same way the workman who sides with one or other of the various political parties against Socialism, does not want to be the slave of capital, never certain of his next week's lodging and food. In coercing him, if necessary, that is, in negativing his *apparent* aims, you are affirming his *real* aims, which are, if nothing more, at least to live in comfort and sufficiency. Yet to grant him the *semblance* of right, the right to perpetuate his own misery through blindness and to deny him the *reality* of right by keeping him a slave —the slave of free contract—this is the object of the Liberal and Radical,—an object he hopes to accomplish by, among other things, flaunting in his face the nostrum of the inalienable "rights" of numerical majorities to control of the executive machinery of the state, at all times and in all circumstances. Of course, as soon as Socialism becomes an accomplished fact, the inert mass of indifferentism which now clings to the *status quo*, not from real class interest, but merely through ignorance and laziness, will be dissolved, and its elements pass over to the new *status quo* of Socialism. The Socialist party will then cease to exist as a party, and become transformed into the absolute majority of the population. Then, and then only, will the right of the majority and the sovereignty of the people be transformed from a sham into a reality— a fuller reality than it ever has been yet.

A few words on one more "idol," to wit on "justice," as embodied in the "rights of property." It is *unjust*, the *bourgeois* will tell you, to nationalise or communise property now in the hands of private persons, since they as individuals have received it in the natural course of things as guaranteed by social conditions present and past. This notion of the right of every man to the exclusive possession of wealth he has acquired without breach of the criminal law, and of the injustice of depriving him of it, is part and parcel of the system of vampire-dogmas and nostrums of which Liberalism and Radicalism are composed. It has been, like the rest, the ideal principle of the middle-class world in its conflict with Feudalism. In the days of the "small industry," the artificer and the merchant asserted this principle in opposition to the feudal lord. The middle-class world affirmed the absolute right of the individual over all his belongings as against the claims of the overlord and his prescriptive dues, as against tenure in fee generally, and above all as against the dearest right of the mediæval baron, the right of plunder and dispossession by force of arms. Security of personal property has ever been the middle-class watchword. Hence this new notion of justice.

In the ancient world it would have been deemed "unjust" for the "tribe," the "people," or the "city" to suffer, so long as an individual citizen possessed aught that could relieve that suffering. In the mediæval world it would have been "unjust" for the inferior to retain aught that his feudal superior required; while in some cases it would have been "unjust" for the rich man to refuse to give alms to the needy. It would have been "unjust" in the mediæval guildsman to have used material of an inferior quality in his work or to have employed more apprentices and journeymen than the rules of his guild permitted. But as we have said, to the corruption and rapacity which characterised the decaying feudal classes at the break up of the mediæval system, the *bourgeois* opposed his thesis of the inviolability of private property and of the ideal of justice consisting in the absolute control of his property by the individual. But, like the rest, this principle unimpeachable as it seemed, had no sooner realised itself, than its reality began to wane. Now, in this last quarter of the nineteenth century it is dead, and stalks the world as perhaps the ghastliest "vampire" of all. The immediate cause of its transition from the living to the lifeless is the change from small individual production to co-operative production,—a change which has reached its consummation in the "great industry." Yet strange to say, the Liberal or Radical can still mouth about the injustice of expropriating the wealthy few for the good of the whole. To him there is no "injustice" in the chronic starvation of myriads of his fellow-men, in the robbery of their labour and health and lives by the rich man by means of his wealth; yet there is "injustice" in depriving the Vanderbilt of a single hundred or the Duke of Argyll of a single acre !

But it is time to drop the curtain on the grim procession. Veritably this last of the bloodless spectres —*bourgeois* "Justice"—will not bear looking on. It is death on the pale horse habited in nineteenth century humbug. The hope and aim of the Socialist must be to lay these troubled ghosts—to consign them to their lower resting-place. Then will "liberty," "equality," "right," and "justice" once more flourish living and real, not in their old forms indeed, which are henceforth for ever dead and meaningless, but in higher and nobler ones. The evolution which we have traced in them through their seeming negation to a higher reality is but one instance of the inherent *dialetic* of the world, in which death and destruction evince themselves the inseparable conditions of life and progress.

IMPERIALISM *v.* SOCIALISM.*

WE seem at the present time to have arrived at
the acute stage of the colonial fever which
during the past three or four years has afflicted the
various powers of Europe. Germany is vying with
France, England with both, in the haste to seize upon
" unoccupied " countries, and to establish " protector-
ates "—the cant diplomatic for incomplete annexation
—over uncivilised peoples. " The rivalry among the
nations for their share of the world market " (to quote
the words of our manifesto) must now, one would think,
have discovered itself to even the casual newspaper
reader as the only meaning the terms " diplomacy "
and " foreign policy " any longer possess. The jealousy
between the courts of Europe, once the sole and until
recently the main cause of national enmity and war,
has in our day been superseded by the jealousy between
the great capitalists of its various nationalities. The
flunkey-patriot, zealous of his country's honour, dances
as readily to-day to the pipe of capitalist greed as he
did before to that of royal intrigue, let it but sound
the note of race-hatred. In both cases he makes the
running for the interested parties. But where the
interested party is the wealthiest and most powerful

* This article was written at the beginning of 1885, for the opening number of the *Commonweal*, the official organ of the Socialist
League.

class, able to pay for "patriotic" articles by the yard,
and "patriotic" speeches by the hour, "patriotism" is
apt to assume the form of a chronic disease. Such it
is to-day, and as such mocks the futile efforts of the
well-meaning but singularly ingenuous clique of middle-
class philanthropists, who are naïve enough to take the
governmental ring at its word when it pretends its
only object in undertaking "expeditions" to be the
rescue of "Christian heroes" or the relief of garrisons,
which have no right to be in a position to want
relieving. War, jingoism—otherwise patriotism—are
indeed past cure while the economic basis of society
remains unchanged, but only so far; and hence
we call on all sincere friends of peace to leave their
tinkering "peace societies" and work for Socialism,
remembering that all commercial wars—and what
modern wars are not directly or indirectly commercial?
—are the necessary outcome of the dominant civilisation. We conjure them to reflect that such wars must
necessarily increase in proportion to the concentration
of capital in private hands—*i.e., in proportion as the
commercial activity of the world is intensified, and
the need for markets becomes more pressing.* Markets,
markets, markets! Who shall deny that this is the
drone-bass ever welling up from beneath the shrill
bawling of "pioneers of civilisation, "avengers of
national honour," "purveyors of gospel light," "re-
storers of order;" in short, beneath the hundred and
one cuckoo cries with which the "market classes"
seek to smother it or to vary its monotony? It seems
well-nigh impossible there can be men so blind as not
to see through these sickening hypocrisies of the
governing classes, so thin as they are.

But we would, above all, earnestly urge the workers
in future to consider "patriotism" from this point of
view. The end of all foreign policy, as of colonial
extension, is to provide fields for the relief of native

surplus capital and merchandise, and to keep out the foreigner. But how, we ask, does this benefit the workers at the best? They are allowed, may be, the privilege of being shipped across the seas, there to help to make the capitalist and land-grabber rich. Some few here and there may, indeed, succeed in a colony which is quite new, in becoming wealthy exploiters in their turn. But the immense majority remain wage-slaves as before. In proportion to the advancing prosperity of the colony—as prosperity is conceived in the world of to-day—is its advancing poverty. Sydney, Melbourne, San Francisco, Chicago, and the leading Australian and New American cities generally, exhibit precisely the same conditions as the cities of the Old World. And how should it be otherwise, since the same causes are at work? To crown dependencies like India, which are held unblushingly as magazines for the aristocratic and middle classes to plunder at their will, it is only necessary to barely allude in a socialist journal.

This, then, is the empire which the blood and sinew of you, workers, are squandered to maintain and extend. With room enough and to spare in the British Islands for all their inhabitants to live a comfortable life, ever fresh lands are sought for exploitation, ever new populations for pillage. It matters not even that colonies already established could accommodate more than a hundred times their present inhabitants; still the vampire Imperialism sucks in fresh territory year by year. Populations to rob and enslave; markets to shoot bad wares into; lands to invest capital upon: to obtain these is the be-all and end-all of modern statesmanship. For this has the stock-jobbers' republic of France waged war successively on Tunis, Madagascar, Tonquin, and China; for this does the thieves' congress sit at Berlin, partitioning the plunder of Central Africa in advance; for this does Bismarck seize Angra

Pequena, New Ireland, and Samoa; for this the sham fanatic and heroic restorer of corrupt Chinese despotism reluctantly (?) consents to go to Khartoum on a pacific mission, collects a body of adventurers on his arrival, proceeds to attack the surrounding tribes, and then shrieks for British troops to protect him; for this, lastly, is Lord Wolseley sent with an expedition in response up the Nile.*

And now a word as to the attitude of Socialists towards the imperial question. For the Socialist the word frontier does not exist; for him love of country, as such, is no nobler sentiment than love of class. The blustering " patriot," big with England's glory, is precisely on a level with the bloated plutocrat, proud to belong to that great " middle class," which he assures you is " the backbone of the nation." Race-pride and class-pride are, from the standpoint of Socialism, involved in the same condemnation. The establishment of Socialism, therefore, on any national or race basis is out of the question.

No, the foreign policy of the great international Socialist party must be to break up these hideous race monopolies called empires, beginning in each case at home. Hence everything which makes for the disruption and disintegration of the empire to which he belongs must be welcomed by the Socialist as an ally. It is his duty to urge on any movement tending in any way to dislocate the commercial relations of the world, knowing that every shock the modern complex commercial system suffers weakens it and brings its

---

* Since the above was written. the Nile expedition has failed, and the Soudan been abandoned. The capitalist found that Khartoum, as a market for white " duck" trousers and Brummagem gewgaws, would not pay for the expenses of keeping, at all events at present. Burmah was found to be a more profitable field for the policy of the capitalist. In consequence King Theebaw became very wicked.

destruction nearer. This is the negative side of the foreign policy of Socialism. The positive is embraced in a single sentence : to consolidate the union of the several national sections on the basis of firm and *equal* friendship, steadfast adherence to definite principle, and determination to present a solid front to the enemy.

THE TWO ENTHUSIASMS.

AN ANSWER TO MR. KARL PEARSON.

IN a pamphlet recently issued,[*] Mr. Karl Pearson has undertaken to assault the fortress of Revolutionary Socialism from the academic side. We are commonly enough bombarded by the professional economist, by the theologian, by the politician, by the "sentimentalist," but the "man of culture" has hitherto confined himself to the drizzling infantry fire of casual criticism. In Mr. Pearson, however, we are bound to recognise an opponent not to be despised, and in his pamphlet a well-planned attack. To drop metaphor, Mr. Pearson, whether he intended it or not, has stated a specious case for the nice young man fresh from the university, who shudders at the "coarseness" inseparable from a real working-class movement, and prefers the attitude of missionary of culture to the benighted proletarian heathen to that of his co-worker in the cause of social emancipation and in the hurrying on of that class-struggle which is its necessary condition. His argument may also to some extent be considered an elaborate justification of another individual, namely of him who really feels that he is essentially unfit for the work of agitation, and that his most useful sphere is in purely intellectual labour, which may quite possibly be Mr. Pearson's own case. We may say at once that so far as we can see, the last-named individual requires no justification at all, since

---

* "The Enthusiasm of the Study and of the Market Place," a lecture delivered at South Place Institute, Finsbury, by Karl Pearson.

Socialists should be the first to recognise diversity of capacity—diversity albeit largely intensified by current conditions—and that the "nice young man" deserves none, save that like the "coarse" proletarian to whom he condescends to direct his missionary efforts, he may plead that he is but the unfortunate result of a vicious system.

With the opening paragraphs of the pamphlet in question, which deal with the distinction between natural and supernatural morality, I heartily agree. Strange to say, on page 3 Mr. Pearson argues for a kind of neo-Puritanism; he would apparently give an introspective turn to social ethics, whereby the attention would still be directed primarily to the formation of individual character, rather than to the clear and broad issues of social life and progress. We may have mistaken the author's meaning, but we must confess the prospect strikes us as rather appalling if the "trivial doings" of each day (let us say, for instance, taking a walk round the room) are previously to performance, to pass the scrutiny of an internal examination as to whether they or the motives prompting them, are "dictated by those general laws, which have been deduced," etc. Certain broad lines of conduct clearly hostile to the existence of social life are to be shunned, other broad lines are to be followed—what more does an ethic founded on social necessity mean than this? Surely, the hair-splitting casuistry of a theological morality, based upon the notion that every action has an "absolute value," and is certain to be rigidly assayed by a heavenly pawnbroker, is out of place here. The resuscitation, too, of that ancient fallacy, that the test of the value or the truth of a doctrine is to be found, not in itself, but in its advocate, I must confess surprises me in a man of Mr. Pearson's ability. His remarks on this head recall to my mind the would-be crushing argument of the Christian advocate of a

generation ago, that Voltaire was a " bad man," and
that hence his attack on Christianity is discredited
at the outset. Also, that the authors of the Gospels
were good men, and, therefore, they were to be believed.
Hegel, we are quite aware, was by no means a man of
heroic moral calibre, but this does not prevent his
reading of the riddle of Life and Knowledge being, not
even excepting Spinoza's, take it all in all, the least
unsatisfactory up to date. As a matter of fact, as
history proves over and over again, there is seldom an
equal balance between the intellectual and moral sides
of a gifted man's character, so that in general we
should naturally expect a man of exceptional power
in the one direction to be deficient in the other.

Turning to the main theme of the pamphlet under
consideration, we find the baneful influence of the
individualistic and absolute ethics which the outset of
the paper led us to hope Mr. Pearson had outgrown
again at work. To the Revolutionary Socialist Mr.
Pearson says, " Abandon agitation, go and create a new
morality." Now, from the point of view of a Scientific
Socialism, he might as well tell the engineer, " Abandon
your borings and your blastings, say to yonder mountain,
depart thou hence and be thou cast into the sea, for
until the ground is level you will never make your
highway." Mr. Pearson is evidently still more than
half a Christian, leastways in his ethics. He thinks
that all social change must proceed from the individual ;
that all reform must come from within, in accordance
with Christian doctrine, but in striking defiance of the
teaching of history and what I may term a *concrete view*
of the nature of things. Morality is with Mr. Pearson
an abstract entity, to be brought to perfection by a
culture of the individual breathed out in some
mysterious manner from the study, and operating by
a magic charm of its own on squalid masses huddled
in recking courts, on the outcast in the recesses of

London Bridge, on the factory slave or the shop-assistant without leisure and resources, on the out-of-work labourer with starvation at his door, no less than on the struggling shopkeeper whose being's end and aim is to hold out against the big capitalist competitor, and last of all on the giant capitalist himself—on the Vanderbilt or the Jay Gould. It is to operate, in short, irrespective of such insignificant obstacles as economic conditions and social surroundings. The factory-slave and the Vanderbilt are alike to feel the renovating influence touch their hearts, to hear the voice of "Culture" and live—a pleasant dream forsooth. Unfortunately, according to Mr. Pearson's own estimate it may take some hundreds of years, and "' while the grass grows——' The proverb is something musty." Mr. Pearson in his study may be content to wait, but will social evolution wait?

"Human society cannot be changed in a year," says our critic. True, answers the Socialist, but its economic conditions can be radically modified in a very few years through the concentration of the means of production and distribution in the hands of a Socialist administration. Thus although one generation may not indeed suffice to complete the transformation of Civilisation into Socialism, yet even one generation may dig the foundation of the fabric, nay, the time being ripe, may even rough-hew its more prominent outlines. We readily admit that the old leaven of civilisation must require many a long decade before it is eliminated, but the generation which for the first time turned the helm of progress in the one direction by which its goal can be reached, would be worthy of none the less honour because it was not itself destined to see the promised land in its fulness. Thenceforward we shall be consciously steering for the goal towards which hitherto we have been at best only unconsciously and vaguely drifting; the whole political and

administrative system, when once the great crisis of the
revolution is passed, instead of, as now, having for its
sole aim the perpetuation of itself and of the class
antagonisms it represents, will have for its end the
abolition of civilisation, that is, of a class-society, and
therewith its own abolition, since with the transformation of Civilisation into Socialism it will be a
superfluous and meaningless survival.

In the pamphlet before us we have once more the
hackneyed argument that the French Revolution left
no enduring creation behind it, that it was abortive
in short. Has Mr. Pearson ever read Arthur Young?
Has he forgotten the state of France before and after
the Revolution? Nay, not of France only, but of entire
western Europe? What was there of human creation
in the French Revolution? asks Mr. Pearson. There
was the creation, at all events, of the supremacy of the
commercial middle class (though there is not much
that is "human" in that, I admit). The French
Revolution meant the final realisation of Bourgeoisdom,
—this was its central idea and purpose,—notwithstanding that it contained episodes which pointed to
something beyond this. Into Mr. Pearson's special
preserve of the Reformation I will not enter particularly, except to say that as I read history a
similar observation holds good there also.

The "enthusiasm of the study" is by no means a
new thing. It is as old at least as Periklean Greece.
In the "garden," the "grove," and the "porch," we
have the enthusiasts of the study; and in the later
grammarians enthusiasts who despised the "market-
place" possibly even more than Mr. Pearson himself.
Yet cannot we date the decline of ancient culture
precisely from the moment when it became the exclusive appanage of the study? This high-toned
ancient enthusiasm of the study, did it make a good
end? Or did it not rather ignominiously "peter out"

in the persons of the seven melancholy and neglected sages or pedants, who wandered in dry places seeking rest and finding none till the worthy Chosroes obtained them a respite for the term of their natural lives wherein to reflect on the vanity of that empyrean "enthusiasm of the study" which had become so rarefied that no mortal besides themselves could breathe its atmosphere? Need I remind Mr. Pearson of other enthusiasms of the study? Setting aside the German humanists, whose work, Mr. Pearson would say, was rendered abortive by the wicked men of the market-place, let us turn to the Italian renaissance, the courts of the Medicis. Here the "enthusiasm of the study" was disturbed by no red-herring of the market-place. Yet what did it effect for mankind at large? What of the French salon-culture of the eighteenth century? For even Mr. Pearson, we suppose, will hardly contend that had it not been for the market-place Revolution which ensued, the "philosophers" and *littérateurs* of the study would have regenerated mankind by the influence of their conversation on the wits, *bons vivants*, and fascinating women of eighteenth century France. "Sweetness and light," again—the refined, æsthetic, middle-class culture of to-day—what has this gospel of "sweet reasonableness" done, what does it bid fair to do? Brought together interesting young men from the universities to study the habits of the East-end "poor," perhaps; provided a temporory stimulus in the direction of soup-kitchens and "literary institutes." Is Mr. Karl Pearson content with such a result?

But the root-fallacy of Mr. Pearson's pamphlet lies, to our thinking, deeper than this. It lies, namely, in his attempt to accentuate the distinction which civilisation has in great part created between the "study" and "the market-place," the man of learning and the man of labour, and to treat it as permanent.

To the Socialist this is merely one of the abstractions produced by a society based on classes, and, therefore, is essentially false and unreal, and as such destined to pass away with the other abstractions—*e.g.*, ruler and ruled, master and servant, capital and labour, rich and poor, religious and secular, etc.—which find their expression in modern civilisation. The enthusiasm of the market-place and the enthusiasm of the study are not properly two things, but one. They form part of one whole. The enthusiasm of the market-place is the direct expression of the particular phase at which social evolution has arrived, the enthusiasm of the study is its indirect expression. The present enthusiasm of the study with the large place modern science occupies in it, differs from the old humanist enthusiasm of the fifteenth century, as that differed from the enthusiasm of the mediæval schoolmen, and so on; and we may add it differs from the enthusiasm of the future, when mathematics shall have been relegated to their due place in the economy of human culture. But the enthusiasm of the study *per se* is no substantial body; though fair in semblance, it is after all but a bloodless wraith. As little can you require the "enthusiasm of the study" to supplant the "enthusiasm of the market-place" in human society, as St. Denis could have expected his decapitated head to urge him on irrespective of the trunk to which it belonged. That the first condition of the healthy animal is a good digestion is a trite observation. The first condition of a healthy society, as certainly, is that it should have something to digest, something besides Pearsonic morality, wholesome as that may be in its proper place. In other words, the intellectual and moral revolution of society rests primarily upon the conditions in which its wealth is produced and distributed. When this is done in the interest of all, and when all take an equal share in it, then that embodied abstraction, the "man of the study," will disappear along with that other embodied abstraction, "the man of the market-place." In a society in which culture is for all, and work is for all, the antagonism of the workman and the scholar will be resolved in the concrete reality of the complete human being. Meanwhile, so long as the antagonism exists, it is plainly the market-place that must create the revolution, since it has the material power in its hands, and this it is which constitutes the enthusiasm of the market-place, unreasoning and "emotional" though it be, the great moving force of society.

THE CAPITALISTIC "HEARTH."

THE throne, the altar, and the hearth—the political emblem, the religious emblem, and the social emblem—have long constituted the mystic trinity to which appeal is made when popular class-sentiment is required to be invoked against influences, disintegrative of the *status quo*. In the *bourgeois* world of to-day the first two terms may be sometimes modified. The middle-class man's respect for the throne *per se* may be more or less diluted; he may even prefer to substitute for it the presidential chair, but in either case it is the "law"—the legal system of a class-society—which is typified; to the altar he might possibly prefer the "Bible," by which he would wish to be understood Protestant dogmas without the inconveniences of direct sacerdotal domination. Such slight modifications of the original phrase as these matters little, however, since in any case the old feudal sentiment for the liege temporal and spiritual has been long since dead. The old formula may, therefore, be conveniently adopted as an indication of the three aspects of the modern world, which its votaries are so jealous of preserving. Beneath throne, altar, and hearth, in their present form, all Socialists know that there lies the market. They know that the market is the bed-rock on which the throne, the altar, and the earth of the nineteenth century rest, and that this bed-rock shattered, the said throne, altar, and hearth will be doomed.

Respecting the throne and the altar we have not

much to say in the present article. It is with the
bulwark of social life, the hearth, otherwise expressed
with modern family-life, that we are here chiefly concerned. We refer more especially to the family life
whose architectural expression is the surburban villa.
This is the ideal of the middle-class family of a
" lower," *i.e.*, poorer degree, while in those of a " higher,"
i.e., richer degree, its characteristics are exaggerated
into the rank luxuriance symbolised in the brand-new
country mansion. Let us consider briefly the characteristics of the suburban villa in its daily life and
surroundings, much as we would that of some ancient
people, as thus :—I. Household Ways; early morning
(*item* 1) Prayers. (2) Breakfast. (3) Departure of
paterfamilias and sons to business. Journey beguiled
by morning papers and conversation resembling for the
most part undigested " leaders" from same. (N.B.
The modern journalist is, as it were, the cook who boils
down and seasons up into a presentable *entrée* the
" dead cats" of middle-class prejudice.) (4) At home
the wife and daughters, after a possible feint at
domestic duties, prepare for " shopping." (5) " Shopping," the main occupation in the day for the woman
of the middle class being over, luncheon follows, then
calls, then afternoon tea. (6) Return of paterfamilias,
more or less wearied with his daily round of laboriously
endeavouring to shift money from his neighbour's
pocket into his own, wearied, *i.e.*, and degraded, with
doing no useful work whatever. (7) Evening taken up
with sleep, or conversation on the affairs of the family,
together with its relations and connections, varied with
the indifferent performance of fashionable music and
the perusal of " current" literature. The above, we
contend, is a fair picture of the type toward which the
daily life of the average English middle-class family
gravitates. We have said English, inasmuch as the
commercial system has been more potent in its effect

on English domestic life than on that of any other
European people; but the same tendency to vapidity,
inanity, pseudo-culture, which is the worst form of
lack of refinement, obtains in one form or another
wherever a commercial middle-class exists. A few
words now on the art, the literature, the sentiment,
moral and religious, of the class in question.

First, as to the house decoration. Not to speak of
furniture proper, what do we see on the walls? Art
embodied in "furniture" pictures, among them oftentimes the terrible counterfeit presentment of connections of the family, which, were there a vestige of
taste left in the household management, would never
be exposed to the gaze even of the casual visitor. The
superficiality of average middle-class culture is pain-
fully illustrated in the complete ignorance displayed
by the middle-class man or woman as to the ugliness
or commonplaceness of his or her relations. We quite
admit that the ancestors or "connections" of a family
may have a certain historical importance for those
interested in its natural history, but, save in a very
few cases, the interest attaching to them is limited to
this. Now, we contend that this does not justify the
obtrusion of what is intrinsically disagreeable. There
is undoubtedly considerable scientific interest in (say) a
well-preserved human abortion, but, inasmuch as there
is that in it which is intrinsically unpleasant, the *savant*
of sensibility keeps it reserved under lock and key for
private contemplation. True "culture" gives a man the
powers of rising above the standpoint of his immediate
interests, and of taking an objective view of things. It
may be too much to expect of a man ever to see himself as others see him, but surely he might see his
relations as others see them.

Apart from portraits, what other art does our middle-
class parlour present? "Reproductions" by processes
varying in badness according to the length of the

family purse. In some instances these mechanical reproductions may be of the old masters, in which case they are perhaps the best thing procurable in the way of art. But for the artist it is surely a melancholy best when art in the family is represented by such. Again, let us take furniture and household decorations. A visit to any large upholsterer's shop will suffice to show the superficiality of the varnish of "taste" in matters decorative, even where absolute sordidness does not prevail. But the English lower middle-class family-parlour, or the never-entered drawing-room of the next grade! Can the "family" which has produced *these things* be in any way worth preserving?

If it be thought that its art and furniture are only superficial, local, and temporary accidents of the modern family, it is only necessary to turn to the rest of its products, to be convinced how very consistently everything connected with it hangs together. Its literature may be divided into two classes—the variable and the constant. The first consists in the circulating library three-volume novel, in which one section of middle-class womanhood delights; the second in "books" designed for "family reading," mostly of a moral or religious tendency, got up in bright colours and gilt leaves, and available at every suburban or provincial bookseller's or stationer's shop, in which another section delights. This class of literature, by the production of which many clergymen of insufficient stipend, and spinsters with disordered organic functions, gain a livelihood, was until the last few years the sole kind certain to be available in the typical middle-class "home." Its way of life, it must be admitted, has fallen somewhat into the sere and yellow leaf of late, but it flourishes more or less still, as the publishing firms of Griffith & Farran, Nisbet & Co., the Religious Tract Society, and even Cassell, Petter, & Galpin, will testify.

Closely connected with this subject is that of religious
practices. Religion in one or other of its forms is
a staple ingredient of *bourgeois* family life in this
country. It constitutes the chief amusement of the
women of the family, who find in Sunday school
teaching, district visiting, bazaars, etc., a virtuous
mode of relieving themselves of the *ennui* which otherwise could not fail to overtake their empty lives. The
singular part of it is, that with all the attempts of these
respectable unfortunates to enlighten and elevate the
" poor," there is an entire absence of all suspicion that
they themselves need enlightening and elevating. Of
late years we note, as a sign of the times, that there
has been a tendency to modification of the teaching
from theology to economy. Evangelicism with its
" conversions," its " changes of heart," has fallen decidedly flat of late, even with that half-educated middle
class, which some quarter of a century ago were its
most prominent votaries. It is tacitly acknowledged
to be out of date. Its catchwords, moreover, now that
they have been dragged through the Salvation Army,
and had to serve as convenient trade-marks for tea,
sugar, and other groceries, and, in fact, make themselves generally useful to the enterprising firm of Booth
& Sons, look decidedly the worse for wear. After the
appearance in a provincial town (as reported in the
newspapers some time ago) of the ingenious advertise-
ment of a Salvation Army meeting, running, " Why
give 10*d.* a pound for mutton when you can get the
lamb of God for nothing ?" the well-known phrase is
perhaps deemed spoiled for the ministrations of the
respectable wife or daughter. There is the possible
danger of getting mixed-up with the " army " and its
proceedings. Be this as it may, the fact remains
that " thrift," " teetotalism," " industry," and the rest
of the economic virtues, are superseding " immediate repentance," " coming to the Saviour," etc., as

the subjects for exhortation in the visitation of the
poor.

But, however unfashionable the old dogmatics may
become, there is one institution which will certainly
hold its own so long as the *bourgeois* family lasts, and
that is the "place of worship." In contemporary
British social life the church or chapel is the rendezvous
or general club for both sexes ; it is the centre, in
many places, round which the melancholy institution
of the suburban or provincial evening party circulates.
It is the *bureau de mariage* for the enterprising youth
who goes to business to qualify for "success in life,"
and the commercial virgin anxious to be settled, to
meet and form connections. Besides all this, it serves
the purpose of a fashionable lounge, where the well-
dressed may disport themselves and make physio-
gnomical observations if that way inclined. So, all
things considered, the "place of worship" may watch
unconcernedly the decay of dogma so long as the
"great middle class" maintains its supremacy—in this
country at least."

We defy any human being to point to a single reality,
good or bad, in the composition of the *bourgeois* family.
It has the merit of being the most perfect specimen of
the complete sham that history has presented to the
world. There are no holes in the texture through
which reality might chance to peer. The *bourgeois*
hearth dreads honesty as its cat dreads cold water.
The literary classics that are reprinted for its behoof it
demands shall be rigorously Bowdlerised, even though
at the expense of their point. Topics of social importance are tabooed from rational discussion, with the
inevitable result that erotic instances of middle-class
womanhood are glad of the excuse afforded by "good
intentions," "honest fanaticism," and the like things
supposed to be associated with "Contagious Diseases
Act" and "Criminal Law Amendment" agitations, to

surfeit themselves on obscenity. And these are the
people who cannot allow unexpurgated editions of
Boccaccio or even of Sterne or Fielding to be seen on
their drawing-room tables! Then again, the attitude
of the " family " to the word " damn." Now, if there
is a honest straightforward word in the English language
—a word which the Briton utters in the fulness of his
heart— it is this word; and precisely, as it would seem,
for this reason it is a word which is supposed never to
enter the " family; " even newspapers, in order to maintain their right of entrance to the domestic sanctuary,
having to print it with a " d " and a dash—the meaning
of which euphemism, by a polite fiction the " wife " or
" daughter " is supposed not to understand. But the
word is coarse and offensive in itself, the *bourgeois* may
retort. You have tried to make it so, I reply, by
classing it with the filthy and inane phrases, bred of
the squalor which modern capitalism creates, but in
reality it is good, expressive English. Nay, more, it
has " higher claims on your consideration "—to employ
one of your own phrases,—it bears the impress of
Christianity upon it; for is it not to Christianity that
we are indebted for the " spiritual significance " of the
word? It was always a puzzle to me why the bare
allusion to a Christian institution should be so offensive
to the ears of the Christian household. In fact, in
common consistency you ought to reduce the " damns "
of your New Testaments to " d——s," to make the work
suitable for family reading. You do not do this, and
why? Because your real objection to the colloquial
" damn " is, as already remarked, that it has a ring of
honest sentiment in it, against which your sham family
sentiment revolts.

Let us take another " fraud " of middle-class family
life—the family party. That ever and anon a wide
circle of friends should meet together in a spirit of
good-fellowship is clearly right and rational; but the

principle of the family party is that a body of persons
often having nothing whatever in common but ties
of kinship extending in remoteness from the defi-
niteness of blood relation to the indefiniteness of
connection—that such a motley crew—should meet
together in exclusive conclave, and spend several mortal
hours in simulated interest in each other. Now a
cousin, let us say, may be an interesting person; but
very often he is not. If he is not, why should one be
expected every 25th of December or other occasion, to
make a point of spending one's leisure with a man who
is a cousin but not interesting, rather than with another
man who is interesting but not a cousin? The reason
is, of course, that the tradition of the "family" has to
be kept up. A "relation," however remote, is, in the
eyes of *bourgeois* society, more to a man than a friend,
however near. So relations, male and female, congre-
gate together on certain occasions to do dreary homage
to this "family" sentiment.

On the same principle the symbolical black of mourning is graduated by the tailor and milliner in mathe-
matically accurate ratio, according to the amount, not
of affection, but of relationship. The utter and ghastly
rottenness of *bourgeois* family sentiment is in nothing
more clearly evinced than in the mockery of grief and
empty ostentation of tailoring and millinery displayed
on the death of a near relation. What is the first
concern of the middle-class household the instant the
life-breath has left one of its members but to "see after
the mourning," as the expression is? Surely, to a
person of sensibility the notion that the moment he
enters on his last sleep his or her relations will "see
about the mourning" may well impart to death a terror
which it had not before, and thus act as an incentive to
carefully-concealed suicide. May not the frequency of
" mysterious disappearances " in middle-class circles be
largely explained by this, without resorting to far-fetched

hypotheses of midnight murders on the Thames Embank-
ment, and the like ? To signify a bereavement to the
outer world (if so desired) by a band of crape on the sleeve
or hat, or some such simple emblem, is one thing; to
eagerly take advantage of the bereavement for the purpose of decking out the person in trousers designed in the
newest cut adapted for the display of the male leg, or
"bodies" in which the fulness of the female breast is
manifested, is quite another, and a very different one.

This, then, is the "hearth," this the family life, the
family sentiment, which certain writers are so jealous
of preserving. In vain do enthusiastic young persons
band themselves together, under the benediction of the
"old man" of Coniston, into societies of St. George, in
the hope that the low level of modern social life, with its
vulgarity, its inanity, and its ugliness, by some wondrous
educational stimulus, emanating from their own enthusiastic and artistic souls, may undergo a process of
upheaval. After some years of Ruskinian preaching, what
is the net result ? A sprinkling of households among
specially literary and artistic circles where better things
are attempted, and so far as the elements of furniture
and decoration are concerned, perhaps with some measure
of success. But even here you commonly find the coun-
terbalancing evil inevitably attending a hothouse culture
out of harmony with general social conditions—viz.,
affectation and self-consciousness. No healthy living art
or culture has ever been the result of conscious effort.
When it comes to saying "go to, now, let us be wise,"
or "let us be artistic," it is quite certain that the
wisdom or art resulting will not be worth very much.
The distinction between an artificial culture of this sort,
which is *cut off* from the life of the society as a whole,
and the natural culture which *grows out of* such life,
is as the difference between a flower plucked from
its root and withering in the hand, and the same flower
growing on its native soil. For what, after all, has

modern art to offer but at best the plucked flowers of
the art of the past, which sprang out of the life of the
past? Your societies of St. George, your æsthetic
movements, etc., only touch a fringe of the well-to-do
classes: they have no root in the life of the present
day; and because they have no root they wither away,
and in a few years remain dried up between the pages
of history, to mark the place of mistaken enthusiasm
and abortive energies. It is surely time that these
excellent young people, together with their beloved
prophet, descended for a while from their mount or
Ruskinian transfiguration, with its rolling masses of
vaporous sentiment, to the prosaic ground of economic
science, and saw things as they are. They would then
recognise the vanity of their efforts, and the reason of
this vanity to lie in their disregard of the economic
foundation and substructure of all human affairs; they
would see the radical impossibility of the growth of any
real art, culture, or sentiment in the slimy ooze of greed
and profit-mongering—in other words, in a society
resting on a capitalistic basis. They would see, further,
that the end of the world of profit and privilege cannot
be attained by enthusiasms, good intentions, or any
available form of class culture, but will have to be
reached by a very different route—maybe through
February riotings, and possibly still rougher things.

The transformation of the current family-form,
founded as it is on the economic dependence of women,
the maintenance of the young and the aged falling on
individuals rather than on the community, etc., into a
freer, more real and, therefore, a higher form, must
inevitably follow the economic revolution which will
place the means of production and distribution under
the control of all for the good of all. The *bourgeois*
"hearth," with its jerry-built architecture, its cheap art,
its shoddy furniture, its false sentiment, its pretentious
pseudo-culture, will then be as dead as Roman Britain.

CIVIL LAW UNDER SOCIALISM.

CONTRACT AND LIBEL.

IT is a common thing for persons to incorporate with their conceptions of a Socialistic state of society elements drawn from the present one, and then to complain of the incongruity of the result. Few persons dream, for instance, that the present elaborate and complex judicial system, or something like it, will not obtain then as much as now. Hence the "difficulties" of so many worthy people.

"Law" is commonly divided into the familiar categories of civil law and criminal law, though legal pedantry could doubtless confound the distinction. By civil law we understand, in accordance with current usage, law concerned with disputes between individuals involving acts which are non-criminal or of which the criminal law takes no cognisance, including all law relating to contract, or the obtaining of damages for injuries, not punishable as criminal offences. It is this department of law upon which we wish to say a few words.

Now we contend that from the moment the State acquires a definite social end—the moment, that is, the machinery of government is taken possession of by, in the name, and for the sake of, the working classes, with a view to the abolition of classes—the whole department of law will become an anachronism which it will be incumbent upon the executive, whatever form it may take, to immediately sweep away. A very little reflection will suffice to show (as the phrase goes) that the civil law referred to is an entirely class-institution, designed (1) in the interest of that class within a class so powerful throughout all periods of civilisation—viz., the legal class, and (2) of the privileged and possessing classes generally. The first point is a trite observation to every one. We all know that "going to law" profits the lawyers more than the litigants on either side. The second point is scarcely less clear. The wealthy litigant is the only person for whom law is even available, for the most part, and certainly the only person for whom it can ever be profitable. The fear of litigation is a weapon society places in the hands of the rich man to coerce the poor man, irrespective of the merits of the case, by dangling ruin before him. If we examine any ground of civil action, we shall find it almost always turns directly or indirectly on a question of property—that is, on what individual shall possess certain wealth—the chances being invariably on the side of the wealthy litigant.

But it may be said, cannot civil law be divested of its class character, and thus serve an intermediary purpose at least in the initial stage of Socialism, when current conditions are still surviving, by constituting the judge, advocate, etc., a mere public servant or functionary, remunerated no more highly than the scavenger? Could not civil "justice" thus be made readily available for all? Perhaps it might, we reply, but it would be anti-Socialistic all the same. Civil law, like all special products of civilisation, is essentially individualistic. It is concerned with the relations of two propertied individuals, one with the other, and as such cannot concern a society established even incompletely on a Socialistic basis. What recks such a society or its administrators of the private quarrels of individuals? Wilful

violence done to any member of society, whatever shape
it takes, is a matter which affects society as a whole—
an offence against society, and hence criminal in kind,
whatever its degree.   But the more or less obscure
question as to who is in the right in a personal quarrel
cannot possibly concern society as a whole.   Two would-
be parties in a civil action, were they to attempt to
inflict their squabble upon a community even so much
as on the way towards being Socialised, would surely de-
serve to be treated in the spirit in which the housewife
possessed of a slop-pail is wont to treat two domestic
cats that plead their causes plaintively upon the roofs
at midnight.   At present, of course, in a state busied in
individual exploitation and scramble for possession, it
matters not that an elaborate machinery is maintained,
involving numbers of persons being kept from productive labour—in other words involving a waste of social
power—for the sake of deciding quarrels; indeed, this
machinery is an essential element in such a system of
society.   For is not the economic corner-stone of this
society, contract, and do not the bulk of civil actions
hinge on questions of contract ?   When contract is part
of the economic constitution of society it is evident its
legal system must take cognisance of contract, for the
observance of contract then affects its existence vitally.
But when contract between individuals is no longer
part of the economic constitution of things such " contract " ceases to have any social importance as to its
performance or non-performance.   "Contract " will then
be understood to be a purely private agreement.   The
community does not ask Peter to trust Paul; he does it
on his own responsibility, and he has no right to come
whining to the delegated authorities of the community
for redress if Paul proves untrustworthy, or to expect
the community to waste resources in keeping up
machinery for the purpose of deciding disputes between
them, with the chances, after all is done and under the

most favourable circumstances, of as frequently arriving
at a wrong as at a right decision.   The principle once
established, that contract rests solely upon honour ; that
any agreement, tacit or avowed, verbal or written, that I
choose to enter into with another man, has no law to
back it—must inevitably have a moral effect in the long-
run of the most beneficial kind.   Civil action concerned
with contract being thus entirely anti-Socialistic in
principle, its abolition ought, we insist, to be one of the
first measures of that people's state whose final aim is to
supersede the State itself by the Society.

To turn now to the case of civil action which does
not refer to "contract," and which probably to many
people nursed under current prejudices will seem of
vital importance to maintain—the action for libel or
slander, to wit.   This "action" is supposed necessary
to the vindication of personal character against attack.
In the first place, the law relating to libel is double-
barrelled, so to speak : it is criminal as well as civil.
But in referring to it I may as well say at once that I
have included both aspects of it.   The ambiguous nature
of its *rationale* is pretty clearly indicated by the doubt
hanging over it as to whether it is directed against
false imputations or any imputations whatever, true or
false.   The law, as far as we understand, technically
covers both ; but the principle of farthing damages and
no costs conveniently obviates the constant display of
the fulness of its absurdity.

No greater or more unwarrantable restriction on
freedom of speech or writing is, to our thinking, con-
ceivable than this law of libel and slander.   We beg
the reader to put aside his prejudices for a moment
and tell us whether it does not bear the most unmis-
takable impress of a corrupt society which it is possible
to have.   The law of libel, look at it what way one will,
seems to be expressly designed to protect the astute
rogue from the most legitimate consequences of his

roguery. Vindicating character, forsooth, in proceedings for libel! Yah! Mr. Belt vindicated his character in this manner, got swinging damages, and a few months afterwards a jury convicted him of a more heinous offence than that originally alleged against him. Every man of the world knows that the successful issue of an action or a prosecution for libel does *not* mean the clearing of the plaintiff or prosecutor's character morally. More often than not it merely means that he is a *clever* rascal rather than a stupid one, or that he has got a clever counsel to represent him. The real *raison d'être* of the law of libel in our hypocritical, hollow class-society is, as already hinted, written on its face: it is a stockade to protect rogues, and behind which every dirty scoundrel can sneak. The "privileged" classes know that their characters in many cases "will not bear investigation," to use the familiar phrase—"shady" transactions in business with neighbours' pockets; "shady" transactions out of business with neighbours' wives. What man of social position—above all, what self-made man—does not owe his position, at some point or other of his career, to something that, were it exposed to the light of day, would constitute a libel for which, in the chicanery of law, he could obtain a verdict with heavy damages against the exposer? This explains the cold shiver with which the proposal to abolish all legal "protection of character" (*sic!*) is greeted by the average sensible man of business. His way of looking at things naturally extends itself to people who have no personal motives to influence them: the tendrils of a sentiment having their root in class corruption ramify far and wide. What every Socialist ought to stand by is perfect freedom of speech and writing so far as personal character is concerned. The Socialist is the last person who ought to form harsh judgments of, or deal hardly with, individuals for their failings; but he ought nevertheless to insist that every man has a right—the advisability or charity of doing so resting with himself —that he has a right, we say, to make known his opinion concerning any other man, be it good or bad, just or unjust, in any way he pleases. We all know that our present class-society—with its commercial and its social rottenness—could not stand for a month the wholesome douche which would result from the withdrawal of the legal protection behind which successful rascaldom skulks, at the first scent of danger discharging its "solicitor's letter" threatening "proceedings."

I have been accused in some quarters of intolerance, because, forsooth, I think that children and ignorant and weak-minded persons (so long as such exist) ought to be protected by society from the ravings of a certain class of dogmatic theologians, even if necessary to the placing of such theologians under physical restraint. Probably the same persons who profess such unbounded *laissez faire* on current lines, and whose Whig ideas of "toleration" are so shocked at the bare notion of any repression of opinion or free speech, even when it means the terrorising or susceptible imaginations to the point of insanity, would wince at the notion of the right of free speech being extended to the opinion that they are morally undesirable persons. The *bourgeois* Radical finds his free-expression-of-opinion principles begin to fit him rather tight here. He finds it is surely most unjust that such an abominable lie should be circulated about him with impunity, when no one that knows him can have the slightest suspicion but that he is a most desirable person—especially morally. Free speech, my friend! Your adversary merely expresses an opinion concerning your actions or your motives. It is open to you to say he is wrong, and to show reason for believing that not you but he is the undesirable person for that matter. What more do you want? Is it "the part" of a magnanimous mind secure in a sense of its own rectitude to wish to persecute the misguided wretch

who presumes to express an opinion derogatory thereto? Of course, given a law of libel we are well aware
an individual may find himself handicapped in not avail-
ing himself of it, since in the event of a direct attack on
his character, if he does not " clear " (?) himself, public
opinion will allow the case against him to go by de-
fault; but this is no argument for the maintenance of
the system. What I contend for is the *right* of every
man to impeach my character, if he cares to, to the top
of his bent, *provided* I have the same right as regards
his. The abolition of legal restraints in free criticism
of character, it is true, might lead at the outset to a
prolific crop of mere malicious slanders. Like a new
toy such criticism might at first be a constant recreation
with some people. But it is easy to see that this would
cure itself in a very short time. Assuming, as will
probably be urged, that every man having a grudge
against another would instantly proceed to circulate the
statement that he had robbed his aged father, and that
his untiring attentions at the bedside of his sick wife
were to be explained by the fact that he was engaged
in administering digitalis in small doses, or that his
solicitude for his niece's welfare masked incestuous
relations, how long would it be before every sane person
had ceased to heed any allegation made respecting another without corroborative evidence? Things having
reached this stage how much longer would it be before
the fashion of making false allegations had died out ?
Even now, who heeds the whispered insinuations made
at election times about the character of rival candidates;
or the many suspicious places in which Mr. Gladstone
or any other public man is said to have been seen.
The very fact of the existence of a law against slander
keeps the practice of slander alive by giving evil insinuations a sting much to the detriment of the man
against whom they are groundless. The slanderer can
always plead the terrors of the law in excuse for not giving

definite shape to his dark hints. He "could an' if" he "would" dilate upon certain things he knows, but prudence compels him to be silent as to any specific charge.

The argument is commonly used, that were "legal redress" for libel and slander removed, physical force would be employed and breaches of the peace ensue. We hardly think the really calumniated would so conspicuously put themselves in the wrong. The employment of physical force against the "allegator" is often strong presumptive evidence of the truth of the allegation. An assault is no answer to a charge—

> "Und könnt' ich sie zusammen schmeissen,
> Könnt' ich sie doch nicht Lügner heissen."

Any scoundrel can commit an assault or get one committed for him, and the legitimate inference is that the intention of committing the assault was only the last resort of an ignoble mind unable to rebut the charge. In any case, personal violence is a criminal offence, to be dealt with as such. The baselessness in reason and inutility in practice, so far as honest men are concerned, of laws against libel is so plain, in short, that they may be taken as the most crucial illustration of the truth with which we started, that they exist, like all civil law, firstly, for the sake of the *legal class*; and secondly, for the benefit of the many doubtful personages that throng the commercial, political, and "society" worlds, but whom it is not convenient to have exposed. They are emphatically *class laws*.

ADDRESS TO TRADES' UNIONS.

ISSUED BY THE COUNCIL OF THE SOCIALIST LEAGUE.

FELLOW-CITIZENS,—

We address you as Socialists. That is a reason, many of you will think, for not listening to us. Socialists, such will say, are unpractical visionaries with foreign notions in their heads, on whom they as practical British workmen have no time to waste. You distrust theories. "Theories are all very well, but they don't raise wages or lower the price of the necessaries of life." You forget that you all of you hold a theory—if not your own, that of the newspaper you read—as to the causes, for instance, of the present depression in the labour market. One will say it is the "wicked foreigner" competing with native workmen; another, it is overpopulation that is to blame; yet another (a little nearer the mark), that it is overproduction. So, after all, the most practical of us does not get on without a theory. The only question is, whether our theory shall be adequate, or whether, even though it contain an element of truth, it shall not, by reason of that element being torn from the whole to which it belongs, be a false, useless, and misleading theory. And we maintain all theories must be this which merely take into account the immediate aspect of a question, without tracing its relation to other aspects—how they act upon it, and how it reacts upon them—and *vice versâ*.

Now Socialism claims to be an adequate explanation

of the present economical facts (and for that matter,
of a great many other things beside, though we are
not concerned with these at present), and also to show
the only way out of the present situation. Very unpractical, you will still think ; but before you make up
your mind to this, we ask you to consider how much
your own practical English methods have done for you;
how much, take things all in all, the working classes
are the better for unionism.

In order to appreciate trades-unionism at its true
value, it is necessary to consider the historic development of the economic relations of which it is the outcome. Let us glance at the condition of the labourer
in the second period of the Middle Ages, when an
industrial system proper first became general throughout Europe—the period of the guild industry. This
was the time when the journeyman, or fellow-crafts-
man, was the social equal of the master, sat at his
table, flirted with his daughters, had the certainty
before him, by good work, of becoming a master in his
turn. The journeyman was but the middle stage in
the life-career of every workman in those days. He
entered the workshop as apprentice; after having
served his time, became the journeyman, fellow-crafts-
man, or "companion ; " ultimately attained the freedom
of the city as the master. Apprentices and "companions," lived together as part of the master's family.
Sundays and the many other holidays the Church
allowed them were spent in healthy social sports and
pastimes, in which masters, journeymen, and apprentices of all trades—the whole body of the citizens—
took part. Then our modern distinctions of classes
did not exist ; capitalism did not exist ; work was
honourable and pleasurable—men produced, primarily
at least, for use and not for profit.

It is true that the privileged classes of those times,
the feudal lords, carried on their exploitation in their

particular fashion : that is, by arbitrary force, whether
it took the form of taxation or of open plunder in the
field or on the highway; but exaction by the fraudu-
lent system of wages, which conceals from the victim
the fact that he is plundered, was unknown.

But a change which was doomed to alter the whole
face of society began to creep into the craft guilds in
the fifteenth century. The proletarian appeared in
the form of the unprivileged workman, who, though
compelled to affiliation with the guild, could never
become a privileged guild master.

In short, the end of this state of society, as of all
other social formations, was destined to come. With
the commencement of the seventeenth century the
change had become apparent, although, as we have
just said, it had begun long before. The old guilds
then either broke up altogether, or else lost all real
significance, like those of London, sinking into meaningless monopolies of wealthy merchants, who guzzle
and drink. The mystic symbolism and archaic craft-
lore were forgotten.

The mediæval town organisation implied the later
mediæval agricultural organisation, the attachment of
the peasant to the soil under a modified feudal tenure.
The decline of the guild-industry is largely traceable
to the expropriation of the people from the land which
threw them in vast numbers upon the towns without
means of subsistence. But the enormous wealth which
the opening up of new markets, and the rise of colonies, enabled individuals to acquire, by the exchange
of home produce, combined with the decay of old
habits of thought, old beliefs, and old customs, to help
on its dissolution.

This dissolution was the negative aspect of the rise
of capitalism. The capitalistic farmer—the farmer
who produced mainly for profit, and employed hired
labourers to help him—appeared upon the scene.

Labour became subdivided. In towns the manufacture system sprang into vogue. The merry journeymen of old now gave place to the prototype of the modern proletarian. The landless, helpless class were ready to serve the needs of the capitalist alike of town and country. Without such a class the capitalist could make no profit, for profit consists in the increase gained in the exchange of the produce over and above its cost of production. But a system like this is impossible so long as the means of production are more or less within the reach of all, as was the case in the simple life of the Middle Ages.

Capitalism—production for profit—presupposes a class of property-holders, who monopolise the means of living, and a class who have only their labour-force to offer in exchange for the necessaries of life. Given this, and you have the conditions of a capitalistic mode of production at hand. With a capitalistic mode of production is given the antagonism of capital and labour so-called, or rather of the capitalist and the labourer. The capitalist, *as* capitalist, *must* seek to lengthen the working day and to keep down wages, in order thereby to increase his share in the product of labour—his profit. The labourer has to defend himself against the capitalist; and he soon finds that the only way he can do this is by organisation. Hence the trades' union. But with the manufacture system capitalism is, as yet, not fully developed. For this machinery is requisite, and the period of the first introduction of machinery on a large scale—of the transformation of the manufacture system into the great industry—a period which falls toward the end of the last and beginning of the present century, affords the material for one of the saddest chapters in the world's history. Every new machine invented has meant, and must mean, the flinging of thousands of men upon the pavement. The action of the "Lud-

dites," in destroying machinery, so far from being a
mere irrational outburst, the result of popular misap-
prehension, as the orthodox economists assert, was
perfectly reasonable and justifiable. Had an insurrection, having for its end the annihilation of these
beauty-destroying, man-enslaving agents, been successful, it undoubtedly would, for a brief period, have
staved off the extreme misery of the workers. But
the ultimate issue must have been the same in any
case. Economic evolution must have had its course.
Steam, machinery was the necessary outcome of the
phase at which production had arrived. The "great
industry" meant the final stage in the development of
the capitalistic system.

Against the iron rapacity of the capitalist, now
completely equipped, labour opposed its organisation,
opposed it in the teeth of overwhelming legal obstacles,
and to some extent successfully. Trades'-unions became a power. But their power was mainly limited to
this country, the source and centre of the economic
movement. Distinctions now arose within the capitalist class itself. The factory lord took the place of the
old working capitalist, who was either driven into the
ranks of the proletariat, or became a middleman or
overseer. The hosts of displaced skilled workmen and
small capitalists who thronged the labour-market
helped to form a reserve army of labour, which was
continually forcing down the price of labour by means
of competition.

The factory-owner now took to the wholesale production of shoddy wares "for the consumption and
enslavement" of the poor. Against this the unions
could, of course, do nothing, though their success, as
above remarked, was at first not inconsiderable, in en-
abling the workers to make headway against the more
direct forms of capitalistic encroachment. This led to
the belief that in the removal of the laws against com-

bination, and the further development of unionism lay
the hope of the workman for the future. Has this
belief been justified? The laws against combination
have been virtually abolished. Unionism is respectable, patronised by Lord Mayors and Members of Parliament. Yet are the working classes the better off?
Is unionism a greater force now than it was thirty
years ago? Does it touch more than the aristocracy
of labour? We think every unbiassed unionist must
answer these questions with an unqualified negative.

Whence, then, the cause of the original success of
the union movement, and of its subsequent failure to
make good its promises? We answer, the original
achievements of the unions were entirely due to the
fact that British capitalists had the fresh run of the
foreign markets, and that the British labour displaced
in the production of commodities was, to a large extent,
employed in making machinery, not alone for home
use, but also for exportation. But foreign competition
has entirely changed the face of things. There are
two well-marked stages in the development of foreign
competition. In the first stage, whilst trade was brisk
and wages high, the foreign labour displaced by cheap
British goods was utilised in this country to keep down
the price of labour. The second stage, which dates
from the general introduction of machinery on the
Continent and in America, is characterised by universal
competition for markets,—a competition which has become keener year by year. As a necessary result of
the scramble, overproduction takes place all round,
the recurrent commercial crises are more frequent and
more prolonged; the earthly heaven of the middle-
class world threatens to become realised in a never-
ending crisis, were that possible. An enormous increase
in surplus labour, owing to the intensified competition, is
the necessary result. To stem this competition trades'
unions have shown themselves less and less capable;

the pressure increases in spite of them. And, be it remembered, the success of unionism lies in its ability to limit competition. So long as trades' unions can effect this they are successful. Their failure to effect it proclaims their rapid decline.

The increase in the employment of women and children, due to the introduction of machinery, and the consequent displacement of men, has now reached a point that threatens to break down all but the most powerful unions. To maintain the same nominal wage a greater and greater disbursement has to be made for provident and out-of-work benefits. (*Vide Statistics.*)

The ratio of unemployed and precariously employed members shows an alarming increase. In many trades the unions are unable to grant continuous relief to their unemployed members. Members are forced, therefore, to compete for work at non-society workshops, and so keep down the average rate of wages. The general result, we repeat, is, that trades' unions do not grow in strength and numbers, but appear to have achieved all they are capable of under present conditions. On the other hand, there is a vast increase in the number of labourers, hucksters, canvassers, etc., etc., who are driven to all sorts of shifts to get a living, and who, from the necessities of the case, cannot become unionists. The unchecked competition among these classes reacts upon the organised bodies and presents an insuperable barrier to any further solid advantage being gained by trades' unions.

The question then now arises, What useful function can unionists still fulfil? We would, in reply, urge upon all unionists to direct all their energies towards consolidating and federating with the distinct end of consolidating themselves the nucleus of a socialist commonwealth—a commonwealth not alone national, but international as well. We urge them to unite themselves with a view, at the earliest possible date, of laying hands on the means of production, distribution, and exchange, in this and every other civilised country, and organising society in the interest of all. To do this, it is needful that political power should be in the hands of those who intend to employ it for the overthrow of the present system, understanding by political power not merely the power of voting, but the possession of the whole administrative system—the complete control of all executive functions. This, then, is the immediate object to be striven for; no mere reforms, be they offered by Tory, Whig, or Radical, will ever permanently benefit the workers. They will but "skin and film the ulcerous place, while rank corruption, mining all within, infects unseen."

Space will not admit of our dwelling on the entire modification of human life generally—habits of thought, beliefs, customs, institutions—which the reconstruction of society on a socialist basis would carry with it. Suffice it to say that this great movement, primarily economical, is no scheme cut and dried; it is a necessary living development of society. The socialist movement is not the coinage of one man, of one body of men, or of one nation; it is the expression at once of a necessary phase of economic evolution, and of a yearning which fills the hearts of the people of all countries and nations throughout the civilised world to-day—a yearning which individuals may formulate, but which no individual can create.

In the general secretary's remarks to the current report of one of the principal unions (the Amalgamated Engineers') a common objection to Socialism is brought forward when it is hinted that under a socialistic *régime* the workman might become the slave of the State. But, friends, we ask you to consider that the great aim of Socialism is the abolition of this bogey—the State, the transformation of the Civilised or state world into a Socialised or communal world.

11

To those immersed in the antagonisms of the current social formation, living its life and breathing its atmosphere, we are aware it is difficult to tear themselves away from them even in thought; we know it requires a mental effort to look forward to that future in which they will have lost all meaning. Yet, without this, Socialism must remain a sphynx-riddle, and Socialists appear the maddest of mankind. If you contemplate the socialist commonwealth as an accomplished fact, you must remember you are contemplating a society in which all are rulers and all are subjects, all are rich and all are poor, all are free and all are bound, and finally in which all relations are religious and all are secular. How shall these things be? you will say.

The good-natured reformer would fain lull such antagonisms to rest by palliatives, make of governing and governed, rich and poor, capitalist and labourer a united happy family, by smooth talk and practical measures. His efforts are vain. We tell you that these antagonisms will never sleep. But though they shall not sleep, yet they shall all be changed. And the change will be accomplished by the very severity of their conflict. A completely collective ownership of the means of production and distribution will necessarily deprive these distinctions, so important in our present social order, of all validity whatever. All will be rulers, since the community will rule itself, the depositaries of the popular will differing in no respect from ordinary citizens, and being revokable at pleasure. On the other hand, all will be subjects, since each will be conditioned by the welfare of the whole. Again, all will be rich, inasmuch as every individual will have the *enjoyment* of the entire stored-up wealth of the community; all will be poor, since no individual will have the *possession* of aught but what he requires for personal use, and the temptation to hoarding will be removed. All will be free, for the artificial restraints of conven-

tion and of law which now rule us will have ceased to
be operative, yet all will be bound to an extent little
recked of to-day—bound by a nobler sense of public
duty, of devotion to the common weal. Lastly, all
relations will be religious, in so far as they have a social
bearing, for the old word which meant devotion to the
ancient city will regain its original meaning, though
with a new light, won through a development of two
thousand years: while all will be secular, for there will
be no class set apart to inculcate the observances and
dogmas of a special creed.

Current antagonisms are thus reduced by their own
exhaustion to the shadows of their former selves, only
to receive a new significance, in which their opposition
vanishes. They are destroyed in their preservation,
and preserved in their destruction. *They are superseded.* We earnestly entreat you, in conclusion, not
to be turned aside by superficial objections, but to read
our literature and judge for yourselves what Socialism
really means, to think over the subject, and when once
you feel convinced, to lose no time in educating, agi-
tating, and organising for the common cause—the cause
of Humanity.

APPENDIX.

———◆———

I.

THE inability referred to in the text, to envisage the past otherwise than with the atmosphere of the present, is apparent in all popular notions of past ages. Exceedingly funny is the unsuspecting guilelessness with which the ordinary politician talks of the English Parliament as having been instituted by Simon de Montfort, as though Simon's war-council were an institution essentially the same, after all, as our House of Commons; or of the compact wrung, for their own purposes, by a band of semi-independent barons, or territorial potentates, from their feudal overlord, called *Magna Charta*, with the unquestioning belief that he is referring to a great popular " measure " similar in kind to Mr. Gladstone's latest Franchise Act only "more so." These belong to a class of historical misconceptions for which language is largely responsible. The same name is used for the most diverse things, simply because there is a thread of historical *continuity* running through them. This *continuity* between the things becomes, in popular conception, confounded with *likeness*, or even *identity*. The term "parliament" or " Commons Assembly " being used both for the casual assembling of feudal estates, for the purpose of supplying their feudal superior with the means of carrying on a war, and also for the modern " representative " institutions of constitutional government, has led the ordinary mind to conceive the two things as

closely connected, if not identical ; whereas, of course, there
is hardly an appreciable point in common between them.
The same class of misconception attaches to the words
"money," "merchant," "usury," "trade," etc. The
ordinary newspaper-reading intellect has little notion that
these words, in past periods of the world's history, when
economical conditions were totally unlike the present,
connote different things to what they do to-day. The
popular conceptions of ancient history and quasi-history,
especially the Bible, are of course the most flagrant
illustrations of what we speak of : these sometimes take a
comical form, such as the Anglo-Israel craze. In this case
of course there is the additional fact that the story of the
rise and fall of the Jewish State is viewed through the
distorting lenses of a theology which has passed through a
long development, and been fundamentally modified several
times, before arriving at that perfect adaptability to the needs
of middle-class Philistinism presented in orthodox Protestant
Christianity. The special unhistorical twist for which this
theology is responsible is, we may mention, often quite as
noticeable in those who reject it—should they happen to
be persons without much culture, such as the average
Secularist lecturer,—as in those who accept it. An
instance of this latter is afforded by what until quite
recently passed for the " Bible-smashers' " special text-book,
and which we were all brought up to regard as the
abomination of desolation,—albeit, to-day its theology is
suggestive of little more, barring its specially eighteenth century characteristics, than the discourse of a mild Unitarian
divine with evangelical leanings,—to wit, Paine's "Age
of Reason,"—and more or less of all writings of which that
is the type. The Bible, to the critical student of history,
contains the indications of a growth of a few loosely-
connected Phœnician or Canaanitish tribes of nomads into
a coherent "people," and thence into a little state ; the
ancestral and tribal cults gradually succumbing to the civic
or national cult which became identified with the worship of
Jaho or Yahveh, established at Jerusalem, the " sacred " city ;
the struggle of this cult to maintain its supremacy over the
other indigenous religions as well as over those imported from

without; its varying success until curiously enough it became associated with the great introspective ethical movement of the prophets, and merged finally into the later Judaism; the whole, with the exception, perhaps, of the last point named, in which the special race individuality comes into play, forming simply a story a thousand times repeated in all essential features in early ages, wherever a " people " has developed a civilisation of any kind. But by the " uncritical " man, whether his bias be theological or anti-theological, the Bible, in its present form, is regarded pretty much as the work of good or bad individual authors, and the whole narrative portion much as the history of a modern state, the prominent actors in which are to be respectively praised or blamed as though they were Lord Salisburys or Mr. Gladstones. It is little suspected that the nearest ana-logue to-day to the Hebrews in their legendary period is to be found in the tribes of the Lebanon or the Soudan. Again, what orthodox English Nonconformist has any suspicion that the Founder of Christianity was other than a kind of sublimated Samuel Morley, in appropriate costume? Could the messianic prophet of the first century, lying hidden beneath the mythical " Jesus," revisit the " glimpses of the moon" in *mufti*, and give his impressions of " the young man preparing for the ministry " it would be certainly edifying. Only the pen of Heine could have given us a suggestion of the result.

The inability of man to interpret the past otherwise than in terms of the world in which he lives has been till the present century universal. Albrecht Dürer paints his Virgin and Apostles as the maiden and burghers of a mediæval German town. So with all the other painters of the Middle Ages. In Shakespeare's " historical plays" the characters live and speak in the world of the sixteenth century. Racine, it has been said, introduced the " manners of Versailles to the camp of Aulis." The suspicion that con-temporary manners and customs or at least contemporary sentiment and ethics, *did* ever *not* prevail has first seriously dawned upon mankind in the nineteenth century. The part cause and part consequence of this flash of insight has been modern " critical " history and " realistic " art. But it is as yet mainly the property of the literary class. To the lack of the historical sentiment is largely due the objection sometimes expressed respecting Socialism on the score of certain *à priori* views on " Human Nature." The man whose sole intellectual stock-in-trade consists in so-called " common sense" (that commodity which is, when highly developed, so very difficult to distinguish from its opposite) finds it even harder to conceive the future save in terms of the present than he does the past. Such a man will sometimes boldly assure you that certain things are opposed to " human nature," the " human nature " he has in his mind being his own, his son's, his next door neighbour's, his wife's, and marriageable daughter's nature. Human nature of course to the student of anthropology and history implies something which has been modified, to a virtually indefinite extent, in the past before it attained the sublimity of smug self-satisfaction expressed in British common sense, and will be still further indefinitely modified in the time that is to come, after British common sense shall have gone to its last rest. "As it was in the beginning is now and ever shall be " may be a very good motto for the *bourgeois* Philistine, for whom both past and future are merely a reduplicated present; but it won't pass muster with any one ungifted with the sound " common sense " and comprehensive ignorance of that individual.

II.

The stage of development of Humanity as a whole must be gauged by the outer edge, so to speak, of progress; that is, by the most advanced indications in the most advanced people at the period; it is in them that humanity is for the nonce most fully embodied and *realised*. They alone give the tone to all the rest. For instance, until about the sixth century the Oriental monarchies represented this " human spirit " (to employ a Germanism), the Aryan races being far behind them. The torch then passed on to South Eastern Europe, which became the head-quarters of advancing human energy. In the Middle Ages the ancestors of the modern races of Western Europe embodied

the active principle of human progress, etc. When once the
particular stage has been reached and passed by the races in
the van of progress—although to attain it they may have
required a long and arduous development—it is henceforth
achieved for all progressive races. The complete evolution
which led up to it having *once* been passed through in its
entirety by the highest group of races at the time being,
can be attained by all less advanced races without passing
through the same development. Thus the economic condition of Western Europe to-day has implied a development
of three hundred years from mediæval conditions. Yet this
does not mean that backward races, in which the level of
production corresponds to that of the Middle Ages with us,
will require at this date to wait three hundred years before
they reach the present condition of Western Europe. They
may easily attain it in ten years. Russia, for instance,
affords an illustration of this. Where but yesterday mediæval
methods of individualist production prevailed, to-day we see
the great industry in its rankest growth. The same with
the intellectual side of things. The most advanced thought
of Western Europe subsists there side by side with the most
archaic superstition. Yet with these facts before their
eyes, writers, who ought to know better, base arguments
respecting the future on the relative backwardness of Russia
at the present moment! The most advanced races, those in
which the *genius humanitatis* is embodied at the time, work out
a development vicariously, so to say, for the rest, who merely
adopt its result. These latter may then easily take the lead
in progress (start a new development of their own) while
their superiors of yesterday fall into the background. This
has been persistently the case throughout history.

Historic evolution, though one *movement*, is not the movement of one people or society, but a movement which passes
through and uses up or exhausts, so to say, whole races one
after the other. Indeed, the races touched by the breath of
the movement of history, while receiving the seal of everlasting life in one sense, that is, as embodying a moment of
historic evolution, receive the seal of death in another, that
is, as actually existent races. The African savage un-
touched by civilisation lives on to-day as he was in Pliny's

time, and as he might be two thousand years hence, so far as internal causes of decay are concerned. But what of the nations of Asia Minor, the Cilicians, the Lydians, the Carians, etc.? What of the Phenicians, the Assyrians, the Hittites? Or, for that matter, what of the classical nations of Greece and Italy themselves, who can hardly be said to survive in their modern representatives? Each race that is drawn into the evolution of human society brings with it, besides its own grade of development, its own ethnical character, that is, the character it has had impressed upon it by climatic, topographical, and other considerations. This is one of the cardinal difficulties in an appreciation of history. Another difficulty is in the many-sided nature of human development. Although unquestionably the domestic and economical aspects of human affairs are the fundamental aspects—although industrial development is their foundation—yet social development is not purely industrial, but political, imaginative, religious, ethical, in addition. Were, for example, the historical order, the exact counterpart of the logical and were the development, a purely economical one taking place in one continuous society, we should find something like the logical process presented. But in the real process of history a particular aspect may be accelerated, retarded, or held in solution at any stage. Archaic, domestic, and economic forms are preserved in religious beliefs and observances, etc.

III.

The best illustration of the "people" stage of social evolution is to be found in the Germanic tribes as they first appear in history, the Catti, the Suevi, the Allemanni, the Rutuli, etc., as described by Tacitus and later writers. The word "*thiud*," meaning people, enters into many of the names of Gothic chiefs and kings, *e.g.*, Theodoric, Theobald, etc. The tract of land occupied by the "people" was the mark. Primitive Communism prevailed amongst them in the time of Tacitus, but the constant state of internecine war, and the tendency to rally round and exalt the victorious leader,

betokened a ripeness for civilisation, which is further
indicated by the tendency to acquire slaves, etc. For
another instance of the "people" the reader may be referred to the early history of the Hebrew race. "What
there was of permanent official authority," says Professor
Wellhausen ("Encyc. Brit.," 9th ed., art. "Israel"), "lay in
the hands of the elders and heads of houses; in time of
war they commanded each his own household force, in peace
they dispensed justice each within his own circle." And
again, "actual and legal existence, in the modern sense,
was predicable only of each of the many clans; the unity
of the nation was realised in the first instance only through
its religion." Herodotus is a rich mine for indications of
the "people" stage. Among modern analogies may be
mentioned the Kurdish tribes, the Arab, and other tribes
of the Soudan, etc. It is, however, I think, important to
remember what has been hinted in the text; that modern
instances of primitive, social, and intellectual conditions
can only with safety be regarded as a more or less close
approach to those conditions of the historical races which
obtained in early ages, and not as some writers insist as
necessarily identical with them. Similarly the modern
anthropoid ape, though undoubtedly presenting in structure
and habits a close analogy with the ape-like ancestor of man,
is not regarded by naturalists as reproducing identically
such ancestor. Just as species have become fixed it seems
likely that races have become fixed. The very fact of the
capacity for development or progress in the "culture-races"
would seem to imply elements in them which from the
earliest stages must have differentiated them from those
"nature-races," where no such capacity exists.

IV.

The "city" was a system of families, gentes, and tribes,
each with a special organisation of its own united together
primarily for objects of production and defence, though
descent from a common ancestor was always assumed for
religious purposes. Every house had its domestic altar for
its family divinities, every division of the city its temple or

altar for the special clan or tribe dwelling within it, while
the city itself possessed a central fane, the largest and most
richly appointed of all for the worship of the city divinity.
The city then was a system of separate governments as it
was a system of separate religions, united together under
one central government and religion. But it was not in
its earlier stages a state in the *full* sense of the word. The
political had not as yet become completely differentiated
from the religious and social. At first the whole society
was the state as the whole society was the church. The
governing body was not external to the governed as it is
to-day. The head of every family was an integral part of
the governing power, as he was of the religious worship.
" *Cité et ville n'étaient pas des mots synonymes chez les
anciens. La cité était l'association religieuse et politique des
familles et des tribus ; la ville était le lieu de réunion, la
domicile et surtout le sanctuaire de cette association*" ("La
Cité Antique," p. 155). " *Ainsi la cité n'est pas un assem-
blage d'individus ; c'est une confédération de plusieurs groupes
qui étaient constitués avant elle, et qu'elle laisse subsister. On
voit dans les orateurs attiques que chaque Athénien fait partie
à la fois de quatre sociétés distinctes ; il est membre d'une
famille, d'une phratrie, d'une tribu et d'une cité*" (*ibid.*,
p. 142).

The city, at first a simple burg, or fortified place, gradually
developed its architecture, etc. As types of the ancient
city may be taken Troy the focus of the great Homeric
epic ; Jerusalem, the focus of the Hebrew epic embodied in
the Old Testament ; and Thebes, the focus of one of the
most important cycles of Greek legend. Curiously enough,
according to the usual supposition, these clusters of stories
(or certainly the first two) arose about the same time (the
ninth century B.C.), and received their final form about the
same time (the fifth century B.C.).

V.

Ancient religion did not concern itself with the supernatural in the sense of a spiritual sphere above, and
essentially distinct from nature. Its prayers were usually

invocations by magical formulæ, designed to compel the will
of the occult or invisible agent to that of the invocator.
That religion in the ancient world connected itself with the
belief in such occult, or in the common acceptation of the
word, supernatural agents and powers goes without saying,
seeing that the whole of nature was conceived as a system
of animated beings. But its concern with this larger system
of nature was always more or less indirect. It was primarily
occupied with human relations—the relation of the individual
with the society into which he entered, of the family with
its gens, of the gens with its tribe, of the tribe with the
people or city. The gods or supernatural agents when they
failed in their protection of the society which practised their
cult were commonly insulted, and their images and altars
thrown down. Religious sentiment did not centre in them,
but in the community whose good or ill was supposed to lay
in their power. The functions of the priesthood of course
involved the knowledge of nature according to current conceptions—*i.e.*, as a complex of occult agencies, in fact, as the
more powerful counterpart of human society. A good
picture of the ancient theocratic priest is given by Flaubert
in Salaambo, in the person of Schahabarim.

The ancient religious cults might perhaps be classified as
follows: first, probably both in order of time and importance, as attaching themselves directly to the society, the
ancestral cults; and, secondly, the *nature cults* proper from
amongst the indefinite number of which two stand out in
respect both of the wideness, amounting almost to univer-
sality, of their diffusion, and of their significance—the Solar
and the Phallic cult. The worship of the traditional founder
of the clan, the tribe, the people, etc., respectively as divine,
is the basis of the ancestral cults; the naïve primitive personification of nature is the basis of the nature cults. Two
of the most striking of natural phenomena to the early
mind, are (1) the sun, the giver of light, heat, fruitfulness,
the cause of the seasons, the bringer also of death, corruption, and devastation; and (2) the generative organs, the
material symbol of social continuity. In the one early man
saw the great principle of external or cosmic life and progress,
upon which society so vitally depended—the fecundating

power in nature; in the other the great internal principle of life
and progress in society itself. Hence the apparently endless
changes the mythologies and religions of antiquity ring upon
these two themes; hence the variety of Solar gods and
heroes—*i.e.*, of personifications of different aspects of the
sun's influence, noxious and beneficent, and the numberless Phallic divinities and symbols with which ancient
religion abounds. Memories of older family and social
forms doubtless also lingered on, and were perpetuated in
religious rites and ceremonies,—a fact which no doubt enters
largely into the explanation of the "sacred prostitution"
of many ancient peoples. The custom or practice dictated
by the social necessities of one age becomes the religious
rite hallowed by tradition of another age, when its necessity
has passed away and its meaning is forgotten, such meaning
having become embodied in other customs and practices.

VI.

It must be borne in mind that production being carried
on mainly by slaves, who formed part of the family of the
citizen, there was practically no exploitation of labour under
the form of "free-contract" such as is the key-stone of
modern capitalism. The "rich man" of antiquity was of
the nature of a *hoarder of treasure.* The notion of increasing
this treasure by means of the process of circulation was
almost entirely foreign to him. His idea was to preserve
it intact, either in the shape of houses, furniture, slaves,
etc., or in that of the precious metals which he would
probably bury. This wealth did not create wealth, except
occasionally in the form of simple and direct usury, for
which, in most cases, the borrower had in the last resort
to pay with his skin, by becoming the property or chattel-
slave of the lender, thus terminating the transaction. The
"rich man" added to his hoard of course when he could,
but the addition was generally altogether independent of the
existent hoard itself. Hence the wealth of the "rich man"
was constantly at hand in a concrete shape to be directly
appropriated. In the disturbances which occurred in some
of the Greek cities,—*e.g.*, Samos, between the rich and the

poor, this hoarded wealth often changed hands in the lump,
so to speak, two or three times. The poor citizens would
rise and drive the rich out, and take possession of their
wealth; the rich would subsequently return in force and
retake their property.

VII.

There is one point in the trite parallel between the circumstances of the execution of Socrates and that of Jesus,
which I am not aware has ever been noticed before.
Long previous to the preaching of an introspective ethic by
Socrates in Europe, the Hebrew prophets had preached an
ethic and religion having the same tendency. After the
exile a compromise was effected between their doctrine and
the older national cultus, which took the form of Judaism,
the poliadic or state divinity Yahveh being erected into
the supernatural god of the universe, demanding a "religion
of the heart," but his national character being preserved in
the "chosen people" theory.

Like all compromises, this illogical position was eventually
assailed. The creed of the prophets culminated in Jesus.
The orthodox Jew sought to combine the spiritualistic
individualism of the prophets with the old civic ideal of
life, of the decay of which this individualism was the sign.
Hence in the Palestine of the Christian era there were two
streams of tendency, one drawing from the tradition of the
prophets, and the other from that of the older priesthood.
The founder of christianity by taking his stand on inward-
ness, personal holiness, purity of heart, etc., and by his
open contempt for the surviving symbols of the old political
cultus, roused the not unnatural resentment of the citizens
of Jerusalem, with whom the old sentiment was naturally
strongest, and for whom the ancient city and temple were
still "holy," and the sanctuary of the fathers; many of them,
indeed, like the Sadducees, caring little for the later tendencies. The result was as at Athens, a conspiracy to be rid
of the blasphemous radical. Thus alike in the crucifixion
of Jesus, as in the death of Socrates we may see illustrated
the conflict between the ancient communist ideal of devotion

to the race, and the new individualist ideal of devotion to the soul, and to its non-natural source. In the "know thyself" of Socrates and "seek ye first his kingdom and his righteousness" of Jesus we have an expression of the same movement, mirrored on the one hand in the logical clearness of the Attic thinker, in the other in the dreamy introspection of the Syrian mystic.

I may take this opportunity of remarking concerning the "community of goods" supposed to have been practised by some of the early Christian bodies, that this cannot be taken by any but the most superficial observer as implying any socialistic tendency as inherent in early Christianity. Like that of the later monkery it is perfectly obvious that the communistic mode of life was a mere accident. It was simply a *means* to another end that end being individual salvation. To avoid the distractions incident to ordinary life and affairs they were abandoned; the individual being thereby better able to concentrate his attention on his soul and "heavenly things." The ascetic motive of course came in as well; the mere self-sacrifice was in itself to a certain extent an end.

VIII.

The exclusiveness of the ancient societies which the Roman Empire and the new ethics combined to break down is almost inconceivable to-day. Each division of the politico-social hierarchy, as already pointed out, was more or less of a closed corporation, a masonic guild, the members of which were bound to each other by the closest of ties, but by ties which had no validity beyond that division. Special religious forms bound a man to his family, others to his clan, others to his tribe, others again to his city, others yet again through them generally of a less intimate and sacred character to the group of cities (the country or kingdom) to which he belonged. There, however, all duty, all sentiment of a common humanity came to an abrupt ending. Beyond the state as federated group of cities, as kingdom or empire, all were Gentiles, outer barbarians, heathen. Such was the inseparability of morality and religion from politics, that a human being outside the political boundary was altogether outside the pale of human relations. The consequence of this negative attitude of the ancient racial morality towards the outer world was rich in consequences,—warfare and slavery directly flowed from it. The conquering power had no duties towards the conquered, and hence its one idea was to utilise them in the interest of its own commonwealth, into which they were therefore introduced. The original political exclusiveness thus paved the way to a social exclusiveness, to the existence of a population within the commonwealth towards which its members owed no duties, and which of course had no rights. Exclusiveness, political and social, may be described as the *negative element* in the system of the ancient world, to the development of which it was indeed necessary, but which, nevertheless, proclaimed its inevitable fall in the very fact of that development— ancient society was strangled by its exclusiveness.

IX.

The two streams, the one traceable to the customs and superstitions of the German tribes, and the other to the Church of the decaying Roman Empire, is clearly visible in the social and religious system of the Middle Ages. Feudalism was as entirely the offspring of the former as Monasticism was of the latter. The " hale young knight," whose " hand was in his country's right, whose heart was in his lady's bower," was as lineally descended from the German of Tacitus, who followed his chief to battle, as the " religious recluse" was from the monks of the Thebaid. Throughout the Middle Ages we can see the true streams of tendency— sometimes uniting, sometimes in conflict. It is quite clear that the acceptance of Christianity by the German peoples could have been little more than nominal. How could the German in the full vigour of tribal life really embrace a religion which placed the highest object of existence in sub-missive suffering, to purify the individual soul, as against that which the early world with one consent regarded as summing up the whole duty of man, namely, fighting and working for the political body? And in fact he did not accept it more than nominally. Duty, lealty to the feudal superior, as representing the community, continued for ages to be the mainspring of his life. Even with the monk, as a general rule, it was the welfare of his order which was uppermost in his thoughts rather than his own personal salvation, as Carlyle has remarked in "Past and Present," and this, notwithstanding that the genesis of Monasticism itself is traceable to a totally opposite sentiment.

X.

The Protestant notion of "reverence" that is, of a special sanctimonious bearing towards things religious, is a direct offspring of that extreme separation of religion from daily life which Protestant, and above all Puritan, Christianity represents. It is nearly certain that the early Christians did not know it, and that their love-feasts were not "prayer-meetings." They were too near to Paganism with its joyous festivals and its conception of a living intercourse between gods and men, to have appreciated the morose priggishness involved in the "reverential attitude of mind" which is *de rigueur* with Protestantism. A religion which really inter-penetrates life does not require the "reverential" pose. *Homo sum, et nil humani a me alienum puto.* Levity is a side of human nature, and a religion that eschews levity by that very fact signs its own death-warrant as a living power among men. I should observe, in spite of what has just been said, that Christianity, without doubt, contained from the first the germ of this sentiment, although it may not have manifested itself immediately; British Sabbatarianism is the hideous abortion it has brought forth.

THE ABERDEEN UNIVERSITY PRESS.

12

www.ingramcontent.com/pod-product-compliance
Lightning Source LLC
Chambersburg PA
CBHW030843270326
41928CB00007B/1190